Contents

SECOND EDITION

EDITED BY

Charles Harmon

NEAL-SCHUMAN NETGUIDE SERIES

Neal-Schuman Publishers, Inc.
New York   London

Some materials in the chapters by Katherine H. Adams and John L. Adams have
been adapted from Michael L. Keene and Katherine H. Adams, *Easy Access:
The Reference Handbook for Writers* (Mayfield, 1999).

The passage from Anna Quindlen's column "Death Penalty's False Promise"
which appears on page 88 is copyright ©1986 by the New York Times Company. Reprinted with permission.

Published by Neal-Schuman Publishers, Inc.
100 Varick Street
New York, NY 10013

The paper used in this publication meets the minimum requirements of American National Standard for Information Sciences—Permanence of Paper for
Printed Library Materials, ANSI Z39.48–1992. ∞

Library of Congress Cataloging-in-Publication Data

Using the Internet, online services, and CD-ROMs for writing research and
term papers / edited by Charles Harmon. — 2nd ed.
     p. cm. — (Neal-Schuman NetGuide Series)
     Includes bibliographical references and index.
     ISBN 1-55570-374-7 (alk. paper)
     1. Report writing. 2. Dissertations, Academic. 3. Research—
Databases. 4. CD-ROMs. 5. Internet (Computer network)
     I. Harmon, Charles. II. Neal-Schuman net-guide series.

LB1047.3 .U75 1996
808'.042'0285—dc21

                                                    00-039441

Contents

Preface

Without a doubt, learning to research and write a paper is one of the most useful skills we learn in school. The process teaches us how to locate information, independently form a thesis, build a logical argument supporting that thesis, support that argument by selecting and using facts persuasively, and present a polished, well-written paper that's prepared for a specific audience. This process prepares us with a strong background for our careers as well as participating in social debates.

When I went to high school, learning how to find the information needed to write a research or term paper meant learning the differences between title, author, and subject cards in the card catalog and how to use periodical indexes like the *Reader's Guide*. Learning how to document information meant remembering where to put the quotation marks in an endnote or bibliographic entry for a periodical article. Compared to learning how to navigate the World Wide Web, download files from America Online, or search the archives of an electronic discussion group, my generation had an easier time researching and writing our papers than do today's students.

On the other hand, the good news is that today's term-paper writer can write interesting papers on a much wider variety of subjects. He or she can locate an almost unlimited amount of information on almost any conceivable subject. The resources available to today's student writers extend far beyond the four walls of the public, school, or university library. Using the Internet, today's students can correspond with experts in almost any field imaginable. They can access materials from the Vatican's library, look at NASA documents, and download whole Supreme Court opinions or Congressional speeches.

Online services also offer a wealth of opportunities for students to explore subject matter from their homes. Whether it's searching a commercial database or using The Electronic Library, students are no longer limited to expensive reference books their parents might or might not be able to provide them. For as little as $4.95 a month, a whole realm of information can come into a student's PC over the home telephone line.

Perhaps the most vital part of the research process today is learning to examine and make judgments about the accuracy and applicability of available sources. While printed reference works typically have been intensively reviewed and the facts they contain verified, electronic resources—especially those on the Internet—may literally be the collected and posted ramblings of one individual. Learning to evaluate sources for authenticity, authority, and currency—as well as knowing how to cite electronic sources—is an essential skill if one is to be information literate in an electronic age. Schools are finally beginning to incorporate information literacy skills into the curriculum at every grade level.

Like its predecessor, this second edition of *Using the Internet, Online Services, and CD-ROMs for Writing Research and Term Papers* combines the best of two traditional generic texts: "how to write a term paper" and "how to use the library." The book's eight chapters are written by two college English professors (who describe effective strategies for note taking, outlining, writing, and proofreading) and three electronic services librarians (who show readers how to use and cite electronic information sources). The contributors' chapters have been arranged so that they parallel the research and writing process.

Throughout the book, readers follow two students, Kristen and Zak, as they choose a topic; conduct research; and write, revise, and polish their final papers (which are presented in Chapter Seven).

Chapter One, "Getting Ready to Write and Conducting Primary Research," covers selecting a topic, setting up a schedule for researching and writing a paper, and conducting primary research such as surveys and personal observation.

Chapter Two, "Secondary Research Using Print Sources," guides students through selecting and using encyclopedias, almanacs, online and card catalogs, and periodical indexes. It also provides tips about gathering information in such a way that it will be efficient to utilize in the writing stage.

Chapter Three, "Secondary Research Using Electronic Research Tools," describes how to choose and search tools ranging from general research sources like the *Oxford English Dictionary* to subject-specific indexes like *ERIC*. The chapter teaches readers how electronic resources "think" so that they can choose good keywords and use them effectively. In a striking variance from the first edition of this text, this chapter now concentrates on selecting resources, choosing keywords, and devising effective search strategies rather than on navigating particular CD-ROMs and online databases. This change (also prominent in Chapters Four and Five) is designed to not only reflect changes in information technology but also to help students develop the ability to use broad classes of information tools rather than becoming dependent on one or two specific titles.

Chapter Four, "Secondary Research Using Online Services," helps students (and their parents) understand what kinds of specialized information and research assistance can be accessed online for a fee. The chapter explores the three major online services that reach the home market (Prodigy, American Online, and CompuServe) as well as more specialized online databases more typically accessed through libraries. One major change reflected in this chapter is its treatment of these services as easily accessible, low-cost gateways to other pay-per-use commercial databases.

Chapter Five, "Secondary Research Using the Internet," begins with a discussion of what the Internet is and how it has changed and grown over the last few years. It then uses screen shots to illustrate how to navigate the Web, link up with subject area experts, and choose and use search engines. Tips for saving time and avoiding less-useful information are also provided. Step-by-step, illustrated instructions are provided for bookmarking useful sites and for cutting and pasting text and images from the Web into research and term papers.

Chapter Six, "Evaluating Information Sources, Writing, and Revising," covers evaluating sources, manual and electronic note taking, and using quotations effectively. Detailed instructions guide readers through developing a thesis, designing an outline, and moving from the first draft through the revision process.

Chapter Seven, "Proofreading and Preparing the Final Copy," helps readers prepare a finished paper that conforms to MLA guidelines. Zak and Kristen's final papers appear at the end of the chapter to illustrate points made throughout the book. Students will especially welcome parts of this chapter that highlight both the benefits and shortcomings of electronic grammar and spelling checks as well as tips for catching common errors.

Chapter Eight, "Citing Print and Electronic Resources," covers the two most commonly used style guides for citing sources: those of the APA (American Psychological Association) and the MLA (the Modern

Language Association). Both basic citation formats and sample citations are given for a wide range of print and electronic sources.

There is almost no resemblance between the electronic tools discussed in this book and those covered in the first edition of this title published in 1996. CD-ROMs, online services, and the Internet are all much more easily searchable. The Internet has totally changed. The first edition of this book discussed gophers and introduced the Web; the primary Internet tools covered in this edition, like Alta Vista, were pipedreams in 1996. What hasn't changed—but is much, much more important today than it was then—is the process of choosing from among all these electronic sources precisely because they are so ubiquitous today. As the chapter on online services points out, subscribing to an online service like AOL can be a very wise choice under certain circumstances because some of these services make databases available at reasonable prices that student researchers couldn't otherwise access.

While *Using the Internet, Online Services, and CD-ROMs for Writing Research and Term Papers* is primarily a guide to researching and writing papers for classes, it also is a guide to becoming information literate—choosing from amongst a wide variety of information resources, evaluating information sources, and then synthesizing and presenting research findings. It is this process that the book stresses and the editor and contributors hope will make navigating the Information Age a little easier.

Charles Harmon

Chapter 1

Getting Ready to Write and Conducting Primary Research

Katherine H. Adams and John L. Adams

When journalists go to the scene of a murder, they ask questions of witnesses and examine the area. At the same time, police collect evidence and medical examiners begin to inspect the body.

These people are "re-searchers," meaning that they search and search again to get a complete picture in order to judge the time of death, type of weapon, and ultimately the identity of the murderer. Such observation and analysis skills are also crucial to the doctor examining a patient, the sociologist observing a community, and the scientist conducting an experiment. To conduct thorough studies and form conclusions, these professionals rely on their own experience and knowledge, on primary research like observations, interviews, and surveys, as well as on secondary research from textbooks, articles, and legal documents.

In your classes, teachers assign research and term papers to help you develop research skills and learn to communicate the results of your work to various audiences. The following sections will help you to choose and narrow a topic for a research paper, to decide on an outline, to write, and to revise. As we proceed, we will review the work of two students, Kristen Hubbard and Zak Cernok, as examples of the research process.

Schedule for a Research Project

complete by

____ 1. Decide on a general topic
and narrow it. (pp. 2–3)

____ 2. Consider the needs of your
readers. (pp. ••)

____ 3. Consider your own knowl-
edge and opinions on the
topic and the needs of your
readers. (p. 3–4)

____ 4. Locate appropriate primary
and secondary sources. (pp.
4–78)

____ 5. Examine the arguments
presented in these sources
and take notes. (pp. 79–83)

____ 6. Choose a preliminary the-
sis and organization. (pp.
83–85)

____ 7. Write a rough draft. (pp.
85–86)

____ 8. Incorporate source materi-
als into your arguments.
(pp. 86–93)

____ 9. Make the necessary revi-
sions. (pp. 93–94)

____ 10. Proofread your work and
prepare the final copy. (pp.
95–110)

PREWRITING

The first step in the research process is to decide on a topic and conduct research concerning it, a step called *prewriting* since this work takes
place before you write a rough draft. This beginning step is perhaps the
most important one because a research paper, whether it concerns AIDS,
Shakespeare, careers, or capital punishment, must present specific information and an interpretation.

Choosing and Narrowing Your Topic

You will first need to decide on a topic you can research and write about
successfully. The following suggestions will help you make your choice:

**1. Pick a topic that interests you or a question you would like
to answer.**
You will enjoy the process more and put more work into your paper if
you choose a subject or question that you want to pursue.

In his civics class, Zak heard a lecture about the death penalty. The
speaker, Sister Helen Prejean, provided data about its costs and its fail-
ure to deter crime and described her experiences visiting with the men
on Louisiana's death row. When his English teacher assigned a research

paper a few days later, Zak decided to use this opportunity to find out more about capital punishment.

If you need help deciding on an appropriate and interesting topic, ask your teacher for ideas, review course readings, or browse the subject headings in your library's online or card catalog or in periodical indexes. Try to avoid settling for an "oh, I guess this will have to do" type of topic.

2. Choose a topic you can research.

When you have decided on a general topic, go to the library to see whether you can find enough material on it. If the information has only appeared in journals that your library doesn't own, if the topic is very new, or if everyone else in the class is writing on the same subject, you may not be able to find enough data. Ask a librarian if you need help with evaluating a possible topic.

3. Pick a topic that is sufficiently narrowed or limited.

If there are entire books on your topic, it may be too broad for a short paper.

Kristen wanted to write on television violence, but she realized that this general topic might be too much to handle, so she considered these more specific choices:

- one Saturday morning lineup or show
- shows aimed at very young children
- toys that enable children to imitate Power Rangers or other favorite cartoon heroes
- the portrayal of boys and girls in adventure cartoons
- attitudes of parents toward violent programming
- immediate effects of viewing television violence

Like Kristen, you may find that scanning book and article titles at the library and discussing possibilities in class can help you decide on a specific topic.

Considering Your Readers

As part of your choice of topic, you should consider the readers of the paper. Will they be your classmates or some other group?

The following questions will help you assess their knowledge and opinions:

- What age are my readers?

- How much education do they have?
- What do they value most?
- What do they fear?
- Will they be seeking my information or will I have to convince them of its importance?
- How do they feel about my topic? How does it affect them?
- How much do they know about it?
- What vocabulary concerning it will they already know? Will their definitions agree with mine?
- What examples will they find most disturbing or inspiring?

Carefully considering the readers' knowledge and biases will enable you to produce a paper that will be convincing to them.

Kristen Hubbard, for example, decided to address an audience of parents on the effects during childhood of repeated viewing of violent television. She thought that parents might compare watching crime shows to playing cops and robbers, a violent play activity of their own childhoods, and thus think of television viewing as being relatively harmless. She decided that she would address this opinion directly in her paper.

Sometimes you will be writing for a more general audience or for the teacher. In these situations, you still should consider the readers' needs and interests carefully. A general audience, or the teacher as the audience, will generally have the following traits:

- They have a general knowledge of politics, history, entertainment, and other fields, but you should not expect them to be experts on your specific subject. Thus you will need to define specialized terminology, explain the historical background of a problem, or summarize the plot of a story.
- These readers will consider your thesis and supporting evidence carefully and critically.
- They appreciate clear, correct writing.

CONDUCTING THE RESEARCH

Once you have decided on a topic, careful "re-search" will enable you to increase your knowledge and prepare to address a reader. This process generally involves *personal, primary*, and *secondary* research.

Personal Research; Experiences You Have Had, Information You Know

Before you begin talking to other people and reading about your topic, consider what you know already. Treat yourself as the first source by jotting down answers to these questions:

- How did I first hear about this topic?
- What judgments have I already made about it? On what evidence?
- What experiences have I had or heard about that concern it?
- What have I read about this subject?
- How do my family, friends, and teachers feel about it?

After you begin working with other sources, you may need to return to these questions—to see if you are changing your mind, if you have begun to interpret your experiences differently.

When Zak answered these questions, he realized that he had always supported capital punishment, but he had based his judgment not on data, but on his feeling that a murder should be avenged. He realized that this emotional response might be shared by his readers, other college-age voters, who could also profit from a more careful consideration of the issue.

Primary Research

Another important research form is primary research, which involves learning by watching what people say and do, asking them questions, and drawing your own conclusions. Primary research methods include *observation*, *interviews*, and *surveys*.

Observation. You should learn to evaluate a situation by analyzing what you observe. To write about hospital care or shopping malls, go out and see what is going on. To write about weight lifting, don't just go to the library: visit a gym.

Before you make an observation, decide on the purpose of the session. Kristen planned to watch cartoons with her younger brothers (ages five and seven) to consider how frequently various types of violent acts occurred, how they reacted to the violence, and how well they comprehended what they had seen. To get this information, she decided to use several viewing sessions and ask them a few questions afterwards.

When you are making such an observation, try to write everything down. You should wait until you organize a rough draft to decide on the importance of your material.

Interviews. Many people may be able to give you a first-hand account of a place or experience relevant to your topic or share their own reading with you. Ask teachers, friends, and librarians for names of such people

When you have chosen an individual you would like to interview, contact him or her, explain your project, and request an appointment. You also might ask if you can bring a tape recorder with you.

Before the session, research your topic and the person you are interviewing. Then you won't waste time asking questions that you could easily find the answers to elsewhere. Next, with the purpose of your interview clearly in mind, prepare a short list of questions or topics.

When Kristen decided to interview a local child psychologist, Dr. Erin Broussard, who was studying television violence, she chose to ask the following questions:

1. On which cartoons do you find the most violence? What age children are they aimed at?
2. Do violent cartoons, dramas, and news shows affect children differently?
3. Do many children repeat the acts that they see on television? Do any particular types or ages of children tend to do so more frequently? Does more frequent viewing lead to more of these acts?
4. Does viewing violence make children afraid?
5. Does constant viewing of quickly moving violent shows lessen their ability to understand complex problems and consider appropriate solutions?

Surveys. To get information from a larger group, like students and teachers at your school, you might decide to create a short survey. Although you could mail these forms, an easier method is to simply hand them out where the group is—to parents at a day care center, to children in their preschool class, or to teachers at a faculty meeting—after explaining your purpose for collecting the information.

To conduct a successful survey, you will need to choose clear and direct questions that will elicit the data you need. Before you administer the survey to your target group, test it on several classmates or members of your target audience to see if their interpretation of each question matches with your own.

Your first questions might identify the respondents by age, job, or gender, whatever information seems important to you. The additional questions, which should not take up more than a page, should be designed so that your respondents don't have to do much writing and so that you can analyze their answers easily: you might use check-off lists, five-point scales, and yes-no questions. At the end of the survey, you can include one or two questions that require a written answer if you want to encourage respondents to express more of their own viewpoints.

To find out what his fellow students thought about capital punishment, Zak designed the survey on page eight.

Capital Punishment Survey

male _____   female _____

1. Do you support capital punishment?
    _____ yes   _____ no

2. If you support capital punishment, for what crimes do you think it should
    be a possible punishment? (Check all those that apply.)
    _____murder of one person
    _____multiple murders
    _____rape
    _____drug dealing
    _____other   Please state:

    _____

3. If you support capital punishment, what are your reasons for doing so?
    (Place a number by all those that apply, using (1) for your primary reason
    and then proceeding with 2, 3, etc.)
    _____It offers the only possibility for the punishment to equal the crime.
    _____It deters crime.
    _____It is less expensive than life in prison.
    _____It makes our community safer since the criminal cannot escape or be
         paroled.
    _____other   Please state:

    _____

4. Do you think that the poor and minorities are more likely than other
    groups to be sentenced to death?
    _____ yes   _____ no

5. What would you most like to tell your classmates about capital punish-
    ment?

    _____
    _____

After collecting the responses, Zak could look at many different issues: whether the students supported capital punishment and why, what information they knew, how males and females differed.

When he reported the data in his essay, he had to state exactly what he had learned: "A recent survey I conducted indicated that 79 percent of 105 male and female students viewed the death penalty as appropriate for murderers, of one person or of several. A much lower number, under 10 percent, viewed it as appropriate for any other crime." He could also quote from the written responses if he indicated that he was citing one opinion.

Secondary Research

Your secondary research will uncover most of the information for supporting your thesis as well as consume most of the time you spend on your paper before you get ready to write. Secondary research using printed sources is discussed in the folioing chapter. Chapter 3 discusses using CD-ROMs to unearth secondary information; Chapter 4 is devoted to online services; and finally, Chapter 5 discusses the wealth of information available on the Internet and the World Wide Web.

You should try to select the best type of source for your particular writing situation. Obviously, if you are writing about yesterday's news, you should use a newspaper or a news service like Yahoo! or America Online rather than a book or CD-ROM. Likewise, an online service probably will not include much information about obscure eighteenth-century painters. Read the following chapters to learn more about a vast array of sources. Then think carefully about the attributes of each kind of source before you spend time using it. If you have trouble deciding where to look for information after reading the descriptions of kinds of sources and how to use them in the following chapters, ask your librarian or teacher for advice.

Chapter 2

Secondary Research Using Print Sources

Katherine H. Adams and John L. Adams

As you collect appropriate types of primary data, you should also turn to secondary sources. Printed materials are one type of secondary sources.

The following sections—on reference works, books, and periodical articles—will help you to use the library effectively.

FINDING BACKGROUND INFORMATION IN REFERENCE WORKS

You should locate several overviews of your subject in reference books. The reference room of your library contains many valuable sources that provide background information and statistical data on almost every subject. You can locate these research tools by finding your topic in the online or card catalog and then looking under the subheading "Dictionaries," by using Robert Balay's *Guide to Reference Books*—a source that lists 10,000 reference books by subject area—or by asking a librarian.

The following sections will acquaint you with some of the most helpful reference tools.

Encyclopedias

You can often find information in general encyclopedias like *Collier's Encyclopedia, Encyclopedia Americana*, and *The New Encyclopaedia Britannica*, which are written for a general audience and cover a wide variety of subjects. But the reference room also contains encyclopedias devoted to one specific field. These specialized encyclopedias, like the ones listed here, provide more detailed background information, an overview of current debates, and bibliographies:

Encyclopedia of Advertising
Encyclopedia of Computer Science and Technology
Encyclopedia of Crime and Justice
Encyclopedia of Education
Encyclopedia of Electronics
Encyclopedia of Psychology
Encyclopedia of World Art
McGraw-Hill Encyclopedia of Science and Technology
McGraw-Hill Encyclopedia of World Drama

Some encyclopedias are also available online and in CD-ROM formats. See the following chapters for information on choosing and using these.

Biographical Dictionaries

Biographical reference works contain brief accounts of well-known figures. To find information about the people who played significant roles in the events you are studying, you might look them up in the following biographical sources:

Current Biography covers persons of various nationalities and professions, providing a biographical sketch, short bibliography, picture (with some entries), and address.

Dictionary of American Biography contains short biographies of over 15,000 deceased Americans representing many professions.

Who's Who in America, *Who's Who* (primarily British), and *The International Who's Who* offer brief biographies of notable living people. The "who's who" label has also been used on a variety of other biographical sources:

Who's Who Among Black Americans
Who's Who in American Art
Who's Who in American Education
Who's Who in American Politics
Who's Who in Economics

Who's Who in Hollywood, 1900–1976
Who's Who in Horror and Fantasy Fiction
Who's Who in Military History
Who's Who in Rock
Who's Who in Television and Cable

Almanacs

For the facts and statistics necessary to substantiate your claims, almanacs are an invaluable source. Their tables, charts, lists, and thorough indexes give the researcher quick access to all kinds of data. Here are two examples:

The World Almanac and Book of Facts. This reference tool contains such diverse facts as the names of sports champions, college tuition costs, and execution totals by state. The almanac covers historical as well as current information.

Statistical Abstracts of the United States. Published by the U.S. Bureau of the Census, this book contains information gathered each year under such categories as Health and Nutrition; Education; Geography and Environment; and Communications.

Dictionaries

The library's unabridged dictionaries enable you to check the meaning of key terms. The *Oxford English Dictionary* explains the derivation of words and their meanings in earlier centuries. Specialized dictionaries, like those in the following list, cover the specialized terminology of particular fields or careers:

Dictionary of Computer Terms
Dictionary of Concepts in General Psychology
Dictionary of Criminal Justice
Dictionary of Ecology
Dictionary of Film and Broadcast Terms
Dictionary of Geography
Dictionary of Historical Terms
Dictionary of Legal Terms
Dictionary of Money and Finance
Dictionary of Music

A Dictionary of Politics
A Dictionary of Science Terms
Dictionary of Television, Cable, and Video

SEARCHING FOR BOOKS

After you have looked in various reference works to get an overview of your topic—and perhaps to narrow it further—you will be ready to use other types of books and periodicals to find more detailed information.

The following steps will help you locate relevant information in library books.

Find the Subject Headings for Your Topic

You will waste time and miss sources if you head straight to the online or card catalog, trusting in your own label for the topic. You first need to consult the *Library of Congress Subject Headings,* found in book form or on microfiche near the online catalog in your library. This guide will tell you what subject headings to use.

If Kristen planned to look under "television violence" or "violence on television," for example, she would find that these labels are not used in online catalogs. Instead, she would need to look under "violence in television." She could also use broader terms like "television programs" and "violence in mass media" as well as narrower terms like "crime in television."

Use the Online or Card Catalog

After choosing the correct subject terms, you will be ready to use the online or card catalog to create a list of books that seem likely to contain information on your topic. If your library's online system is new, all of the older books may not be listed on it. Ask a librarian if you will need to use the card drawers to search for older books.

The catalog lists books by author, title, and subject heading. For most searches, you will be relying on the subject heading entries, which begin with Library of Congress subject labels.

You can save time—and find the best materials—if you study the entries carefully. Each card or computer entry, like the sample given below, contains a great deal of information that should help you decide whether to choose a book or not.

Search Result -- Quick Search

Viewing Record **6** of **77** from catalog. There are also <u>cross references</u>.
❏ Check here to mark this record for Print/Capture

HV8699 .U5 C67 1997
Just revenge : costs and consequences of the death penalty /
Mark Costanzo. Costanzo, Mark.

Personal Author:	**Costanzo, Mark.**
Title:	**Just revenge : costs and consequences of the death penalty / Mark Costanzo.**
Edition:	**1st ed.**
Physical descrip:	**xiii, 206 p. ; 22 cm.**
Publication info:	**New York : St. Martin's Press, 1997.**
Bibliography note:	**Includes bibliographical references (p. [171]-197) and index.**
Held by:	**MAIN**
Subject term:	**Capital punishment--United States.**

Here are some of the questions you should ask about each potential source. You may not be able to answer all of them, but the answers you generate will help you decide whether the book will be worth locating:

- **Author's Name:** Do you know who the author is? Have you read or seen entries for other books by the author? Is he or she a well-known expert? Mark Costanzo, for instance, is a psychology professor at Claremont Graduate University and a member of the editorial board of a journal, *Law and Human Behavior.*
- **Title:** Does the title seem related to your topic? *Just Revenge: Costs and Consequences of the Death Penalty* seems to question the fairness of the death penalty and to focus on problems created by capital punishment.

- **Date of Publication:** When was the book published? A 1997 book about capital punishment probably would be more useful than one written in the 1960s for many reasons, including changes in the way many states implement the death penalty.
- **Page Numbers and Inclusions:** You might want to note the length of the book and whether it contains illustrations, a bibliography, and an index.
- **Subject Headings:** You should also note the other subject headings where the book is listed because they may lead you to additional books on your topic.

If you are using an online catalog, you may also be able to find out whether a book has been checked out.

Even if you only need three or four sources, record or print the information about every book that seems relevant to your topic. You will save time when you begin looking for books if you have a long list of choices.

SEARCHING FOR PERIODICAL AND NEWSPAPER ARTICLES

While you are finding relevant books, you should also search for pertinent material from magazines or journals. "Magazines" refers to *Newsweek, Sports Illustrated,* and other general reader periodicals that might be sold at a newsstand. Journals—like the *Journal of Social Issues* or *The New England Journal of Medicine*—contain scholarly articles intended for experts. Both types of publications are called periodicals.

You should look for periodical articles because they contain recent scholarship about very specific subjects. By checking both magazines and journals, you can choose articles aimed at different readers and thus obtain various perspectives on a topic. For a daily news perspective, you might also want to use stories from major newspapers.

Use Periodical Indexes (Both Printed and Computerized)

To find periodical articles on your subject, you will need to use an index. You can search printed indexes, CD-ROMs, or online databases to locate titles, abstracts, or—in some cases—articles themselves that relate to your topic.

The *Reader's Guide to Periodical Literature,* which you have probably used before, primarily lists magazine articles under Library of Congress subject headings. To locate more detailed, scholarly articles, you will want to use specialized indexes, also found in the library's reference room. Many of them look like the *Reader's Guide*, but they contain entries from journals in one specific field. Some specialized indexes also have short summaries, or abstracts. The following list will give you an idea of the specialized indexes that are available:

> *America: History and Life*
> *Art Index*
> *Biological Abstracts*
> *Business Periodicals Index*
> *Communications Abstracts*
> *Criminal Justice Periodicals Index*
> *The Education Index*
> *General Sciences Index*
> *Humanities Index*
> *Index Medicus*
> *MLA International Bibliography of Books and Articles on the Modern Languages and Literatures*
> *Music Index*
> *Social Sciences Index*

With printed indexes, you have to look for your topic in each annual volume. But some of these indexes are also available on computers, allowing you to search several titles at once for articles published over several years and print out the bibliographic information and abstracts for what you find.

Almost all libraries now have periodical databases on CD-ROM (Compact Disc-Read Only Memory) that are updated regularly. If your library has Wilsondisc, you can search any of the Wilson indexes, like the *Reader's Guide, Humanities Index, Social Sciences Index,* or *Business Periodicals Index.* Your library may also have InfoTrac I or II, which indexes business, technical, legal, and general periodicals as well as *The New York Times.* (Chapter 3 covers electronic resources in detail.)

In addition to CD-ROMs, many libraries also provide access to computer networks linked by telephone connections. The Internet is a huge network linking libraries, businesses, the government, and individuals, enabling you to gain immediate access to indexes and online periodicals. Dialog Information Retrieval Service, an information service, allows you to use more than 300 indexes. SearchBank and FirstSearch both provide abstracts and sometimes entire texts of general interest articles and more specialized writings, such as those related to health issues or consumer products. Other popular computer database providers include ORBIT, BRS Information Technologies, and Mead Data Central. Ask your librarian to help you with these online services and to explain any charges that you may incur in using them. (Chapters 4 and 5 provide additional information on online services and the Internet.)

Whether you find entries through a computerized or paper index, you will want to examine them carefully, by looking at the author, the title of the article, the title of the periodical, the length of the article, the date, and certainly the abstract if one is available. You should also find out whether your library receives the periodical and what call number it is listed under: libraries either provide a printed list of their periodical holdings or they include entries for their periodicals on the online catalog.

Check Newspaper Indexes

Newspapers provide day-to-day accounts of historical events. Their editorial and living sections can also acquaint you with the opinions and habits of earlier eras and different places. Most major newspapers, like *The New York Times* and the *Washington Post*, have printed and online indexes. Your local newspaper may also have a printed or online index. And some online services include full articles. For instance, FirstSearch provides some stories and features from *The New York Times* online.

GATHERING YOUR SOURCES

With a preliminary bibliography compiled, you will be ready to locate your sources. You can check in the lobby or the reference room of the library to see what call numbers are found on what floor. Some newer magazines and newspapers may be in a reading room; some of the older ones may be on microfilm.

Here are a few tips that can save you time when you are collecting materials:

1. **Make sure that each source has information that is relevant to your topic.** Before you check out a book or copy an article, do a bit of prereading. First, check the indexes to make sure that the book contains information on your topic. Then quickly scan the cited pages to decide whether the information is relevant. You can then take home—or photocopy pages from—only those books that will be helpful. Similarly, you might scan a periodical article or study its abstract and introduction before deciding to copy it or read the entire piece.

Also, check to see if these sources mention other ones that you might want to locate.

2. **Browse the shelves near the books you have come to get.** Since books are shelved by subjects, the ones nearby may also be pertinent to your topic.

3. **Plan for documentation.** If you photocopy parts of articles or books, write down the publication information (author, title, date, publisher, volume, and page numbers) on the copy itself and staple the pages together. Then you will have this information when you begin compiling a list of sources. (See Chapter 8 for help with documentation.)

Chapter 3

Secondary Research Using Electronic Research Tools

Sarah Sheehan-Harris

This chapter covers the best ways of using traditional library resources like encyclopedias and journal indexes that are accessible in an electronic format. You have probably learned about using encyclopedias and the *Reader's Guide to Periodical Literature* in their book formats in school. Many encyclopedias and indexes like the *Reader's Guide* are now available on CD-ROMs and the World Wide Web (WWW). While this availability can make doing the research for your paper both easier and a little more fun, electronic information can create information overload.

One way to prevent information overload is to search only research-related CD-ROMs and WWW sites. Searching more popular sites can waste your time and get you sidetracked. Research CD-ROMs, such as encyclopedias, dictionaries, and handbooks, can be found in your school or public library. You may even have one at home if you (or your parents) purchased a computer recently. Many of these tools are also available on the Web.

This chapter will help you learn to choose the appropriate kind of research tool, choose effective keywords for searching, and make good choices about which information you want to actually retrieve.

DECIDING WHICH ELECTRONIC REFERENCE TOOL TO USE

Reference tools, such as the *Oxford English Dictionary* and the *Encyclopaedia Britannica,* are found in most libraries. They are also found on CD-ROM and the WWW. Unlike the book versions, which are set up alphabetically and allow you to flip through each volume, the electronic versions, whether on CD-ROM or the WWW, use commands to find information. Although searching electronic reference tools is becoming easier, you will definitely need to allow yourself additional time when using them for the first time.

Before you begin using the electronic resources available in your home, school, or library, you first need to decide what kind of information you want to retrieve. If you're looking for general background, historical, or biographical information, you should begin with an electronic encyclopedia. If you're looking for current information, you should begin with journal indexes or databases.

The first step to finding articles for your research is to understand the requirements of your assignment. Before you begin searching a journal index, be sure you have determined the answers to the following questions:

- What is my topic?
- How long is the research paper supposed to be?
  (The time required to research a five-page paper is much different than the time required for a ten-page paper.)
- What kinds of sources am I expected to use? Which source should I NOT use?
  (The type of sources you may use indicates the types of databases you may search.)
- How many sources am I required to use?
  (The length of the paper and number of sources needed helps you determine how many article databases you may need to search.)
- When is the assignment due?

Here is an example of answers to these questions. Notice that the response is *specific*.

I need information on the effects of *pollution* on *global warming* for a *five-page paper* for my English class. I have to use *three scholarly sources.* I may also use books and popular magazines. I may not use electronic encyclopedias. Also, I must have *two Web sources.* The paper is *due after midterm* (which is about six weeks away).

Writing your answers out helps you plan your strategy before you start selecting your electronic research tools. For example, using electronic encyclopedias for the paper in the above example would be a waste of time since they are not an approved source.

USING ELECTRONIC ENCYLOPEDIAS

Electronic encyclopedias are wonderful research tools! Not only do they contain the actual articles found in the print version, but they also may have additional pictures, video, and audio. As computers become more sophisticated with sound and video features, so are the electronic encyclopedias. Now you can see and hear John F. Kennedy deliver his inaugural address, instead of just reading it. Another benefit to electronic encyclopedias is cost. They are usually much less expensive than the print versions. If you already have an electronic encyclopedia, you have your first electronic reference tool.

Electronic encyclopedias tend to be self-explanatory. If you have trouble using one, try accessing the help feature. If that doesn't answer your question, ask your librarian for help.

One tip you might find helpful is using your mouse to copy material you are going to quote (with appropriate attribution, of course) into your paper. This saves time and avoids typographical errors.

USING ELECTRONIC RESOURCES TO FIND JOURNAL ARTICLES

Searching research-based WWW sites may be harder than using electronic encyclopedias. Your school or public library may subscribe to a general topic journal index database on CD-ROM or the WWW. A journal index will list magazine articles on a particular subject and tell you what magazine the article is in. Using a journal index is much faster than flipping through 52 issues of *Time* magazine for an article you thought you read a few months ago.

The electronic journal index will produce a list of articles based on the specific search you enter. Usually you will see the complete citation for a journal article and an abstract or summary of the article. More and more electronic journal indexes can also provide you with the full text of the online article. All you may need to do is print it out.

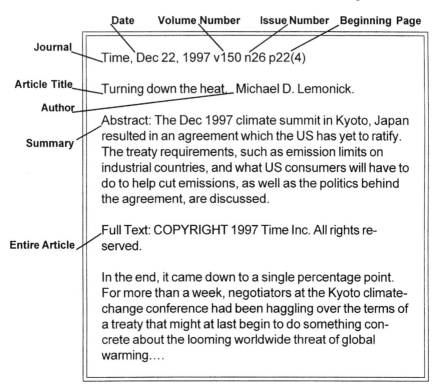

Date   Volume Number   Issue Number   Beginning Page

Journal — Time, Dec 22, 1997 v150 n26 p22(4)

Article Title — Turning down the heat. Michael D. Lemonick.

Author

Summary — Abstract: The Dec 1997 climate summit in Kyoto, Japan resulted in an agreement which the US has yet to ratify. The treaty requirements, such as emission limits on industrial countries, and what US consumers will have to do to help cut emissions, as well as the politics behind the agreement, are discussed.

Entire Article — Full Text: COPYRIGHT 1997 Time Inc. All rights reserved.

In the end, it came down to a single percentage point. For more than a week, negotiators at the Kyoto climate-change conference had been haggling over the terms of a treaty that might at last begin to do something concrete about the looming worldwide threat of global warming....

General Citation Indexes

Three common indexes you may find easily accessible and particularly useful for your research are:

Expanded Academic Index (also known as Infotrac)
One of the most popular WWW journal indexes available. *Expanded Academic Index* contains citations to all of the articles it indexes, as well as abstracts and some full-text articles.

Periodical Abstracts (also known as Proquest)
This is also a very popular journal index that is available on both CD-ROM and the WWW. It also has citations to all of the articles it indexes and abstracts, and full-text to some of the articles.

Readers Guide to Periodical Literature
This was once the most popular print journal index and your library most likely still receives the print version. *Readers Guide*

is also available in a CD-ROM version and on the WWW. It only contains citations and abstracts.

Subject Specific Journal Indexes

A full-text or general citation journal index may *not* be the best resource for every topic you write about. There are over 500 journal indexes available electronically, but only a small number contain the full text of articles. If the full text is not available through the index, you will want to make sure the actual article in the journal is available to you. Always check with your librarian to make sure you are using the best electronic journal index for your topic.

Subject specific indexes usually list scholarly or professional journals. Some of the most popular ones and the subjects they cover are:

DATABASE	SUBJECT COVERED
ABI-Inform	Business
American History and Life	History
CINAHL	Nursing
Engineering Index	Engineering
ERIC	Education
INSPEC	Engineering and computer science
LEXIS/NEXIS	Current events, legal, and business
Medline	Medicine
PsycInfo or PsychLit	Psychology
Sociological Abstracts	Sociology

HOW TO BEGIN A COMPUTERIZED DATABASE SEARCH

Conducting Your Search

Once you've chosen which electronic research tools to use, you're ready to search for information.

Computerized databases, whether they're CD-ROMs or Web-based, search for information in specific ways. To effectively use electronic journal indexes you need to know how they work. They do not deal very well with a search term like "I need information on global warming for my English paper." You have to identify specific terms that define your topic. These terms are usually called *keywords* and are used by the computer to search for information.

Remember the terms relating to the topic that was presented in the section on determining which research tools to use (see page 22)? *Global warming* and *pollution* are the keywords that define the topic.

Not every computerized journal index uses the same keywords to identify the same topic. You may have to try several alternatives to your keywords to find the right information. Take some time to identify possible alternative terms so you are ready if you do not get good results with your first keywords.

> Alternative keywords for *global warming:*
> ozone layer
> greenhouse effect
>
> Alternative keywords for *pollution:*
> acid rain
> emissions

Once you have selected the electronic journal index you wish to search and identified a number of keywords, you may be faced with two different ways to begin your search. The first is a *subject* search and the second is a *keyword* search.

Subject Searching

Limits the term(s) you enter to the subject field only. So, if you don't know the specific subject the database wants you to use, you may not find any journal articles on your topic.

Keyword Searching

A much easier way to search than subject searching. Depending on the specific database you select to search, the keyword search will look for your keywords in the:

- title of the article
- title of the journal
- abstract of the article
- full text of the article
- words in the subject heading list.

It is usually easiest to begin searching using a keyword search.

Note: The instructions **for searches** may differ slightly depending on the database you are using. Read the help screens on the computer or ask for help at the reference desk in your school or library.

The keywords you've chosen may mean absolutely nothing to a computerized database. When you type in a keyword the computer searches the database only for the *occurrence* of that keyword.

Here is an example using the database called *My Favorite Recipes*. Let's say you are in the mood for pasta and you want to find recipes in the database that use pasta. Your keyword is **pasta**, so you type it in and perform a keyword search.

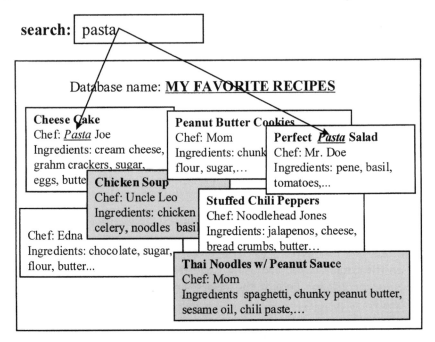

The results of your search will be a list of **all** recipes that have the word **pasta** (Cheese Cake and Perfect Pasta Salad), regardless of whether it is an ingredient or the name of a chef or whatever. But the results of your search will leave out the recipes for Thai Noodles and Chicken Soup, both of which have pasta as an ingredient. Why? Because the pasta in those recipies is listed as **noodles**, not **pasta**. Your keyword search only asked for occurrences of **pasta**. This is a good example of how your choice of keywords will affect the results of your search and illustrates why you should always think of alternative keywords.

CORRECTLY ENTERING YOUR SEARCH

When you are searching using two keywords, every electronic journal index will ask you to put an **AND** between the two (or three or four) words. **AND** is an operator used to *narrow* the number of articles you find. Using **AND** requires both keywords to appear in the articles.

Do not use a **+** sign or the word **in** or **effects**. Using these operators to narrow your search will not work.

Looking back to the *My Favorite Recipes* database, here is an example of a keyword search using the **AND** operator and the results it would produce:

SEARCH

> ### Keywords: noodles AND chili

RESULTS

> **Thai Noodles w/ Peanut Sauce** (*because* noodles *appears in the title and* chili sauce *appears in the ingredients*)

Remembering the terms relating to the topic presented in determining which research tools to use (see pages 22 and 26), here is another example of a keyword search using the **AND** operator:

SEARCH

> ### Keywords: global warming AND pollution

RESULTS

> *Congressional Quarterly Weekly Report,* June 5, 1999 v57 i23 pS8 Setting Priorities And Paying The Tab. Mary H. Cooper.
>
> Abstract: The US has made significant advances in controlling **pollution** since 1979, yet the next phase of environmental action will need to address the complex issues of **global warming** and widespread air **pollution**. A majority of Americans responded to a Gallup Poll and another by the Sierra Club in giving environmental concerns priority, yet economic impact from treating **pollution** crossing state borders has yet to be assessed.

Use the operator **OR** to *expand* the results of your search. **OR** means the results will have *any* of your keyword terms in the article, title, author's name, etc.

Here's an example of a keyword search using the **OR** operator:

SEARCH

> **keywords: pasta OR noodles OR spaghetti**

RESULTS

> Cheese Cake (***Pasta*** *is the chef*)
> Perfect Pasta Salad (***pasta*** *is in the title*)
> Thai Noodles w/ Peanut Sauce (***noodles*** *is in the title and **spa-
> ghetti** is an ingredient*)

Remembering the global warming example, here is another example of a keyword search using the **OR** operator:

SEARCH

> **Keywords: pollution OR acid rain**

RESULTS

> *Science*, Nov 6, 1998 v282 i5391 p1024(1)
> **Acid Rain** Control: Success on the Cheap. (decline in **acid rain**) RICHARD A. MKERR.
>
> Abstract: **Acid rain**, once a major environmental concern, is a declining worry as the causing chemical agents have been reduced in half. Controlling **acid rain** was projected to cost the government up to $10 billion a year, but has been surprisingly cheaper at a cost of $1 billion a year.

Kristen and Zak could find an incredible amount of information for their papers using journal indexes, but encyclopedias probably wouldn't yield much useful information because both their topics require current information on social issues. Kristen could use the keywords **television and violence** to retrieve only article citations that include both of those keywords. Zak would use the **OR** command in a search string **capital**

punishment or death penalty to retrieve articles indexed with either of his two key phrases.

Using an electronic resource can reduce the time you spend researching a subject, but the first time you search online make sure you have plenty of time to learn the database. Just because one database has full text doesn't mean that it is the best place to search. If you are unsure how to begin searching, ask a librarian.

Chapter 4

Secondary Research Using Online Services

Lara Bushallow

Generally speaking, fee-based information services are economically feasible only to the experienced researcher who knows which database to choose and what search strategy to use. While powerful, searching the specialized database requires experience, a well-planned outline, and deep pockets; access to most databases, such as full-text newspapers, business information, and full-text journal or magazine articles include additional charges that can add up quickly.

In contrast, Internet Service Providers (ISPs) make it easy to get online by distributing free software and trial subscriptions. The software may even come preinstalled on your new computer, requiring only a credit card and a modem for immediate access. Anyone can follow the wizard instructions to set up the ISP of their choice in a matter of minutes. Little, if any, technological knowledge is needed. Even when such knowledge is needed, help files and an Internet glossary are often included to assist you. Local ISPs can grant you access to the Web with little assistance or support. For a fee, as you will see below, you can find customized software and search features that makes what you are looking for on the Web much easier to find. Most of the research sources that are discussed in this section can be found at your local library for free, in print or electronic format.

This chapter explores the three major online services available to households, Prodigy, America Online, and CompuServe. It then describes some online databases commonly found in libraries.

PRODIGY INTERNET

Prodigy Internet gives you direct, high-speed access to the Internet. It is easy to install and requires little more than a credit card to get started. In general, it is easy to navigate and allows users to instantly access the Internet upon dialing in. Prodigy allows you to use Netscape or Internet Explorer as your default Web browser, which is helpful if you are already familiar with either browser. Overall, if you are willing to pay for research, Prodigy is effective for finding articles related to business, health, entertainment, science, and current news events. Prodigy pre-selects Websites to ensure reliable and useful content for your research needs and organizes the content into sections for you to effortlessly find what you are looking for.

General Features

The design and layout of Prodigy's homepage is logical. The convenient tabs "My Home," "My Favorites," "Shops," "Prodigy Extras," "At Work," and "Help" enable you to find the information that you are looking for quickly and easily. Advertising is kept to a minimum, which can keep online time down, and general information such as headline news, stock information, and weather forecasts are at your fingertips. The "Tools for Living" section on the far right side of the screen directs you to helpful research tools and other items of interest. This section allows you to choose either the "channel" method of navigation or the search/keyword method. The search box feature allows you to use Prodigy's JumpWords, a specific list of keywords from Prodigy, or the Excite search engine to find what you are looking for. Prodigy indexes more than 50 million Websites in its search engine, including more than 10,000 recommended or evaluated Websites, and over 300 Web-based publications. These recommended Websites are pre-selected by Prodigy staff based on content and reliability.

News

Prodigy Internet serves as a gateway to a variety of news sources. One of Prodigy's strongest features is AP Online and the integration of news sources on its home page. You can get up-to-the minute U.S. and International news as soon as you login. Late-breaking news is accessible from the Prodigy main page, while other headline news can be found under the "news" channel, on the right side of the screen, or by entering "News Community" as a JumpWord. The News Community provides you with access to sources such as ABC News, CBS News, MSNBC, AP Online News, and CNN. Prodigy's software suite includes RealPlayer, Shockwave, and Flash Player, which allow you to take advantage of the live broadcasts and other mediums that CNN Interactive and other news sites broadcast.

Full-text coverage varies throughout the news sources. Some sources require registration in order to search for information while others are free to search but charge a fee to obtain the full-text article. The dates of coverage also vary from source to source, some being 14 days and others several years.

Research

Selecting the "Education" channel and then "Reference" guides you to a list of resources including biographies, dictionaries, thesauri, encyclopedias, libraries, maps, news, periodicals, health, legal, and business. Each choice reveals a list of "Recommended Websites" and "More Sites." In general, the "Recommended Websites" are free and some include reviews. Access to well-known encyclopedias such as *Grolier's Academic American Encyclopedia, Encarta*, or *Compton's Interactive Encyclopedia* requires individual subscriptions. Prodigy Internet provides a means to access these services, but the cost is generally not included in your monthly ISP fee. Depending on the amount of use, it may be cheaper to buy the CD-ROM rather than pay the monthly service fee. The *Encarta Concise Encyclopedia* is available at no extra charge.

The Business Reference Center (use the Prodigy JumpWord "Feature" to get to this source) is a fee-based service provided by WinStar Telebase Inc. This easy-to-use service provides access to a variety of sources from one location. The main page is arranged by subject: Business and Company Information; Copyrights, Patents, and Trademarks; Medicine; News; People and Biographies; Science & Technology; Social Science; Government; and Education. Each subject area is further divided by categories with the available databases listed for each category.

A few of the research sources included are: Dun & Bradstreet, Moody's U.S. Corporate News, Major U.S. Newspapers, PsycInfo, Dissertation Abstracts, Encyclopedia of Associations, and U.S. Patents full text. The cost per search and retrieval varies for each source as does the cost to view each full record once you have found what you are looking for. Fees are anywhere from $0.50 to search to $89.00 to retrieve a U.S. Supplier Evaluation Report (SER). Full-text newspaper articles are typically $0.50 to conduct a search and $2.00 to obtain the full text. Again,

Prodigy is merely acting as an access point to this service, which is accessible to anyone searching the Web through any service provider as long as they are willing to register and pay the stated fees.

Homework Helper

Homework Helper, also known as the Electric Library, is a fee-based service to which Prodigy serves as a gateway. The Electric Library is an easy-to-use research tool that requires a monthly or annual subscription fee with unlimited access to its resources. Homework Helper is an online library containing thousands of articles from magazines, newspapers, news wires, transcripts, and books (i.e., encyclopedias, almanacs, history books, classic texts, poetry, etc). It also includes over 40,000 photos and images, as well as hundreds of maps. It is updated daily.

Searching the Electric Library is free. Using either Boolean commands (AND, OR, and NOT) or natural language searching you may search for information on your topic from a variety of sources, or select a particular source type. For instance, you can choose to search for your topic in newspapers and newswires, but not in books, TV and radio transcripts, or magazines. Homework Helper's search engine searches all of the stored text for the provided words.

Results are displayed in a detailed or condensed format and may be sorted by relevancy, date, reading level, or size. When the results are displayed, icons are also used to denote source type. Each entry is given a relevancy score based on a scale of 0 to 100. You can use the power setting to adjust the search power to low or high when using the natural language search option to increase or decrease the search engine results. You can also limit the maximum number of documents that may be included.

Search results may be downloaded for offline access or printed for future reference. Full citations are provided for each article. Homework Helper is straightforward and easy to use and covers a wide variety of subject areas. Most of the sources are from popular journals, daily newspapers, and general interest magazines. The help section is useful not only on how to use the Electric Library's many features, but also on how to prepare yourself for research and the entire research process, including evaluating the results and citing the sources.

Besides cost differences, there are other subtle differences between the databases available through the "Business Reference Center" and the "Homework Helper." For example, if Kristen used this tool for her paper on television violence, she could enter into the "Business Reference Center" and select PsycInfo, under the Social Science Resources, and search for scholarly articles in journals with references and footnotes, chapters of books, dissertations, etc. Since PsycInfo uses a thesaurus, possible subject headings or descriptors might include television viewing and violence. Results would include such sources as the *Journal of Comparative Family Studies* and *Aggression and Violent Behavior.* Although "free text" searching is available, this database allows for sophisticated searching enabling the researcher to limit to particular fields for more relevant results.

A search in the Electronic Library, using the terms **television violence** would retrieve references from ABC Nightline, the *Washington Post, US News & World Report,* and the *Christian Science Monitor* to name a few. These sources would be timely and up-to-date but would be limited in historical background and studies. The link to "Find Related Internet Sites" could prove useful to Kristen as long as she evaluates each site carefully, particularly for originating source or affiliation site and author or person responsible for providing the information.

Finally, Prodigy, like many other service providers, allows you to create a customized page, which can include only those sites that you frequent most often, making your research that much easier. The benefit of using Prodigy is that it is very user-friendly. You will save yourself time by eliminating a lot of the irrelevant sites that you might otherwise receive from conventional search engines when conducting research via the Web.

AMERICA ONLINE

Founded in 1985, America Online, Inc., is the leading Internet Service Provider. America Online, Inc., is also the parent company to CompuServe. With more than 17 million subscribers and growing, America Online (AOL) already has a European presence and is expanding internationally.

AOL attracts many users with its easy-to-use interface, powered by Microsoft's Internet Explorer browser. Some users find the service unattractive because of the number of additional screens that appear when you login, including advertisements, a "Welcome" screen, the "Channels" window, "Your Buddy List," and the "AOL Search Preview" window. To turn off the network news broadcasts you must go through a series of steps under the "My AOL" tab. Nonetheless, you will still be confronted with all kinds of advertisements throughout the site.

American Online is useful to persons of all ages and is especially good for novice users, although you need a lot of patience while waiting for windows to either open or close down. Regardless of the number of windows that are open, there seems to be a long delay in connecting to a service within AOL itself. If you choose a service plan with a limited number of hours, you can waste a lot of time just waiting while being charged extra for exceeding the allotted hours each month.

Getting Around

If you have the default set, the Channels window will automatically appear on your screen at some point when you first sign on to America Online. You can use this feature to jump to a specific subject area or enter a keyword in the "Find" box. You will also have a number of smaller windows open on the screen as well as a very colorful main menu toolbar to assist you in where you want to go. Like Prodigy, America Online has a list of keywords that will take you to specific areas. These keywords are basically shortcuts to your favorite places online. In the middle of the toolbar you will see the keyword search box. You can also type the URL of a Website such as *www.cnn.com* in this text box to go directly to that Website. Most AOL areas have a keyword assigned to them. "KEYWORD" always appears in the lower right corner of the window that is opened.

AOL's major area of interest, Channels, includes AOL Today, News, Sports, Travel, Research and Learn, Work Place, and so on. Within each of these Channels you will find a list of references to choose from. A word of caution: each time you choose a subcategory, another window opens on the screen. When using the "Find" option in the "Channels" window you can also enter a keyword. One particularly user-friendly aspect of AOL is the way keyword searches are configured. An alphabetical list of keywords can be found be clicking on the "KEYWORD" icon on the toolbar at the top of the screen. The keyword function is not case sensitive and therefore very forgiving. URLs may even be entered in all capital letters.

General Features

America Online 5.0 has a short online video to get you acquainted with their service. If you have been an AOL member before but have not seen the latest enhancements, it will introduce you to all the new features.

E-MAIL

AOL's e-mail interface is not in the least bit complicated. If you never sent a message to someone before through America Online, you would be able to easily figure it out. The large icons on the right-hand side make it easy for you compose and send a letter, even offline if you wish to. You are able to send messages using various font sizes and colors and you can even include an attachment.

INSTANT MESSAGE

This feature allows AOL members to have instant, private communication with someone who is online with AOL at the same time as you are. This will allow unwanted clutter in your current mailbox.

AOL LIVE

AOL Live allows you to chat online with celebrities, well-known personalities, and authors. Interviews are conducted online, topics are debated in real-time, and you can join in anytime you choose. AOL Live is America Online's largest gathering place, capable of accommodating thousands of guests.

CHAT ROOMS

Arranged by broad topics of interest, these "rooms" allow AOL members to simultaneously share ideas with people from all over the world. To enter into a chat session, first select the "People" icon, then choose "Find a chat," choose a category such as "Town Square" or "Arts & Entertainment," and finally click "Go Chat." You must type your message in at the bottom of the window. Sometimes chat rooms do fill up and you are offered another selection in the meantime. Audio sounds may be utilized in chat rooms. To hear sounds played in chat rooms, simply choose the "My AOL" icon, and then select "Preferences." In the "Preferences" window, click "Chat," and finally check "Enable chat room sounds."

MESSAGE BOARDS

Also known as discussions groups or newsgroups, message boards are similar to bulletin boards where one can post messages, comments, questions, or responses to whomever at any time. Grouped by topic, you may choose to read or post messages to other AOL members. Unlike chat rooms, there is no need for real-time interactivity. You may also select the newsgroups you want and read them offline.

AUTOMATIC AOL

Automatic AOL, formerly known as Flashsessions, allows you to go online to send or retrieve e-mail, newsgroup messages, or download files that you have previously stored.

Research

America Online provides the usual general reference sources that can start you on your way: encyclopedias, dictionaries, directories, and so on. To access these sources, AOL members may enter the keyword "encyclopedia," for example, in the "KEYWORD" text field or choose "Channels" and then "Research and Learn" to see a complete list of sources. Encyclopedias included in AOL's basic subscription package are *Compton's Encyclopedia* and the *Concise Columbia Electronic Encyclopedia,* in addition to many free subject-based encyclopedias that are found on the Web.

AOL does have numerous resources for teachers and students alike, but not for the avid researcher. Most of the AOL "Channels" refer you to forums, which include information uploaded from a variety of sources including AOL members themselves. The "Search and Explore" option is even divided by the following audiences: Students K–12, Adult Students, Parents of Students, and Knowledge Lovers. One resource that each of these subdivisions eventually points to is the Electric Library, which is a fee-based retrieval service for full-text articles and reports. If you are willing to pay for your research, then you will be satisfied with the Electric Library's results.

The Electric Library, or eLibrary in AOL and mentioned previously in Prodigy's "Homework Helper," offers reliable information at a cost. There is no need to wade through endless, irrelevant links from the Internet looking for the information you need. It is simple to subscribe to this up-to-date "online library" that offers more than 150 full-text newspapers, hundreds of full-text magazines, newswires, maps, photographs, and over 2,000 books on current and historical events. Special versions of the Electric Library are also available for K–12 schools, public libraries, academic institutions, and corporations. (*www.elibrary.com*) Advanced search options allow you to limit searches by author, title, source type, publication, or date. This source is geared toward students of all ages who need a minimal amount of information, at a reasonable cost, in a short amount of time.

The Electric Library is particularly safe for younger children. Unlike searching the Web, parents and teachers know exactly the type of information and content that is stored in the database. It is similar to materials found on your local school or public library's shelves. The current pricing plans are $9.95 per month or $59.95 per year.

Zak could find magazine and newspaper articles for his paper on capital punishment by using the Electric Library on AOL. After logging in and choosing the "Research and Learn" channel, he would then select "Electric Library @ AOL." Zak can then type **"capital punishment"** or **"death penalty"** as his initial search statement. The results display citations from various sources, such as magazines, newspapers (both national and international), dictionary entries, and news transcripts. Zak may choose an article from *Criminal Justice Ethics*, the *Dictionary of Cultural Literacy*, *USA Today*, or *Talk of the Nation* (NPR). The time period for the above search covered 1997 to the present. If Zak wishes to modify his search statement, there is the option to "refine" the original search using another term or he may enter a thesis statement or phrase. A search on **"does capital punishment decrease crime"** results in a very different list of results than the first search.

America Online does provide access, or a gateway, to information that other ISPs do not have rights to. AOL has gained exclusive access to certain "services" such as full-text magazines *George Online* (keyword: George). The "KEYWORD" feature can save you time *if* you know that a particular source exists in AOL, but it is not easy to keep up with all of them. When all else fails, take a guess and enter any keyword. If you are just beginning to gather information on a topic, be patient while seeking resources in AOL. A recent search in the "Research and Learn" channel required multiple clicks to get to a single source that then allowed me to search for my topic.

Here is a sample search done from the perspective of trying to find a topic, and then information on that topic, in preparation for a history class assignment. I decided first to search by the "Channels" feature since this is the latest feature. I chose "Research and Learn." Looking over the list of subcategories, I saw "History." From there I was able to narrow it down to "History–American" and then the Civil War forum. Once there, I found a library, or "archives," containing pertinent software, photos, and biographies. Files placed there by other AOL members have descriptions of what the file may contain, who the author is, when it was uploaded, and what type of program is required to read or view it should you choose to download it for your research needs. There was also the Civil War Information Center that contained the *Civil War Journal*. Additionally, there were links to selected Civil War Websites, AOL Net Find, a Civil War Chat Room, and related AOL Forums. In general, I was able to find a few articles about particular battles that took place during the Civil War, complete with copyright statements and a cited source.

While searching through the Civil War information I came upon a page that referred to the keyword "Web Centers." Entering "Web Centers" as a keyword led me to AOL's Website that "organizes the Web for you," allowing you to search the Web for your topic in a structured format. There is a section called "Time Savers" that included two "research pathfinders." One was entitled "Research an Illness" with links to support groups, advice, medical libraries, and so on, and the other "Research Your Family Tree" which contained guides and advice, public records, genealogy communities, Internet genealogy databases, and a link to the National Archives in Washington D.C.

If you are still looking for information you can visit the "News" channel. This is a neatly organized section that contains over 77,000 articles. You can find top stories, *The New York Times* on America Online, CBS News, and *Time.com*. There is also an extensive list of regional newspapers under local news. News is updated continually and sources include: the Associated Press, Reuters, Bloomberg, Business Wire, PR Newswire, and SportsTicker. Articles are kept online for a minimum of three days. The search feature within "News" allows you to search by keywords and Boolean logic, exact phrases (use single quotes around the phrase), and adjacency, i.e., George W/1 Bush, George W/2 Bush.

The "Newsstand" also offers National Public Radio (NPR) and a variety of magazines depending on which News Channel you pick: Computing, Business, Entertainment, Sports, Workplace, etc. A brief listing of publications are: the *Atlantic Monthly*, *Business Week*, *Columbia Journalism Review*, *Congressional Quarterly*, *National Review*, *The Christian Science Monitor*, *Financial Times*, and *The Sporting News*. News Channel essentials is an added feature that allows you to search for news by topic, by country, "Find your Elected Official," "E-mail Congress," "Track Officials' Votes," and "Take a Poll."

America Online does offer a good place to find general information. It is aimed at families and students who need access to a wide range of topics, especially in high-interest consumer subject areas such as health, business, and current news. The resources are arranged by broad topic areas and provide a lot of "how-to" information for its users.

COMPUSERVE

CompuServe (CIS—CompuServe Interactive Services) is a subsidiary of America Online, Inc., and is one of the oldest ISPs. CompuServe has over 2 million members (*www.compuserve.com/corporate/cs_info.html*) worldwide. It offers access to more research databases than either

America Online or Prodigy. After being sold to American Online, Inc., CompuServe has tried to market itself to a more specialized clientele rather than the general consumer.

CompuServe is easy to install and the monthly rates are comparable to other major commercial online services for basic service. CompuServe offers its members a simple communications program but the Web interface, like America Online, uses its own software. The Windows-style terminal interface that appears within the browser is limiting and does not allow you to copy or print what is in the window every time. The response time is extremely slow even though there are not that many graphics or advertisements.

Getting Started

The main menu is organized to allow you to move easily through the many services that CompuServe provides. You may search the Web, access your e-mail, visit a chat room, or access the status of your account online. The menu choices on top also allow you to always find your favorite places, search CompuServe, browse the Internet, check the weather or stock quotes, or review a history of what you have done since you logged on.

There are several ways to navigate through CompuServe. You may choose from the list of five main categories or services: What's New, Table of Contents, Internet, Chat, or Forums & Communities, or use the "Go" or "Find" features and directly enter in what you are looking for. The Table of Contents icon will take you to a list of "channels" similar to AOL and Prodigy. Channels include such topics as News, Research, Health & Fitness, Business, and Arts & Entertainment. The channel approach leads you through a maze of choices that uses a split screen to display the information. The left side of the screen typically includes a text list of related topics and the right side includes graphical icons on broader topics that may interest you. As you make your choices the text list continues to change on the left side of the screen. It is not aesthetically pleasing but it is simple enough to use.

Like Prodigy and AOL, CompuServe uses a jump feature for users to access the information they need quickly and easily. The "Go" feature is the quickest way to move between services. All you need to do is click on "Go" or press Ctrl-G and enter the service that you are looking for. If you do not know the name of the service, or the abbreviation (MagDB is the abbreviation for Magazine Database Plus), you will only get so far. If you use the "Go" index you will then be able to search for a topic of interest, download a list of all CompuServe services, or read the overview on how the index works. The list of services is extremely long and having to download the list instead of viewing it makes it awkward to use.

The "Find" icon allows you to search CompuServe services by topic or subject. Once you enter a word, a list of services that relate to that topic will be displayed with the name of the "Go" word to the right. You may then double click on the item you wish to visit or add the service to your favorite places.

General Features

Although CompuServe has a monthly charge allowing unlimited access, there are premium services that carry surcharges above the flat rate. Charges may apply to searching databases to retrieving newspaper articles. You will usually see "Pricing Information" in the list of choices when accessing databases that incur additional charges. You are notified of charges after you have completed a successful search.

Some free features of CompuServe are Chat, E-mail, and Forums. Chat allows members to communicate with one another in real time. You can participate in public chat rooms, group chat rooms, or private chat rooms. Most rooms are devoted to particular topics but you may choose to just gather some friends and chat in a group chat room. Forums and communities allow members to discuss topics via chat, post messages to message boards, and even share files, software, graphics, and so forth with one another. There are over 1,500 forums in CompuServe at the moment.

CompuServe offers an encyclopedia and dictionary to help you begin your research. By choosing the "Go" icon, located in the top-center part of the screen, and entering encyclopedia in the pop-up box, you will be directed to the Grolier Multimedia Encyclopedia. Grolier contains over 30,00 articles and 5,000 pictures. You may also access the Merriam-Webster Online Dictionary by simply entering dictionary.

DATABASES

CompuServe has more resources than AOL or Prodigy. Using the "Table of Contents" icon from the main menu and then the "Research" channel you can find literally hundreds of popular and scholarly resources at your fingertips. After choosing a research tool, you will find a common list of summary instructions for each source, including Description, Search Guidelines, Pricing Information, and Help Files.

IQuest, a list of hundreds of databases on any subject—business, health and general magazines, newspapers, executive news service, Dow

Jones publications library, and research news—is the largest premium database service that CompuServe has to offer. Additional charges do apply when searching and retrieving the actual information from each of the databases. A running total is kept during your session. If you are not careful, your bill can grow quickly.

Help screens are available for each database, which can make your searching more effective and thus less costly. Surcharges vary per database but due to the sheer number of databases it is always best to check the pricing before you search. To download a full-text newspaper article, for instance, would cost you $1.50, but to find the article you might pay $0.50 just for the search. At these prices, your research can turn out to be a very costly venture.

Over the past few years, ISPs have grown ten-fold. Although the large commercial ones have remained, they have changed considerably with the expansion of the World Wide Web (WWW). Prodigy, America Online, and CompuServe are ISPs and not information or data providers. For the most part, they are all in competition with free, reliable information sources already available on the Web. The major difference is the price you pay for organization and content. Consumer online services offer you a package that makes accessing, navigating, and searching the Web a whole lot easier while also providing technical support, e-mail, and chat rooms. Emphasis is on service not product. Consumers are looking for convenience, speed, reliability, and ease of navigation when using the Internet, whether it be for research, e-mail, newsgroups, or chat.

ONLINE DATABASES

There are literally thousands of online databases available for research. Depending on the level of research, you may need to consult individual vendors to subscribe to a database or service that meets your needs. Databases can be multi-disciplinary or very specialized. Some databases have complex search commands that require training to be effective in retrieving the information you are looking for. The complexity of a specialty database may be enough to discourage someone from using it, not to mention the cost. So the commercial services discussed above are a good alternative for the novice researcher.

Numerous vendors that have provided libraries and professional researchers with database services over the years. Using the changing technology, these vendors have been able to mass market their products directly to the research community. Gone are the days of having to schedule an appointment for an online search at your local university or public library. With the rapid growth of the Internet, many databases are available to the average researcher simply by walking into a library and getting on the Web. Libraries subscribe to these same services at a much lower cost. Although assistance may still be required, it makes it easier for the end-user to do the searching themselves.

Dialog, a leader in online information, provides access to the full content of over 400 databases containing 330 million articles, abstracts, and citations. Subject coverage is comprehensive and most databases go back to the early 1980s in coverage. Bluesheets are still available for every Dialog database to assist you with your searching. It is highly recommended that you review the bluesheet of each database before you begin your search. The current standard usage plan requires a minimum monthly fee of $75.00 in addition to the initial sign-up and membership fees. Unless you wish to be an expert in Dialog, it is not practical to subscribe to this service for casual research needs. For more information, visit *http://products.dialog.com/products/dialogweb/index.html*

Lexis/Nexis has been around for many years and is well known for its news and legal information. The expansion of the WWW has enabled Lexis/Nexis to diversify its clientele. Services are now tailored to the academic community, the business community, the legal field, and government professionals. Whether you are looking for a full-text newspaper article, a court case, or a market report, Lexis/Nexis puts it at your fingertips. For more information, visit *www.lexis-nexis.com/lncc*.

InfoTrac Web, from Gale Group, Inc., is another full-service product for your research needs. Compared to Dialog and Lexis/Nexis, this product is in my opinion the easiest to use and provides just enough information for the average researcher. It covers a variety of subjects and reference sources and includes full-text articles and images. For more information, see *www.informationaccess.com*.

Chapter 5

Secondary Research Using the Internet

Frederick D. King

The Internet is a worldwide network of computer networks linked together by a common communications protocol, known as TCP/IP. It was developed in the 1960s by the United States Department of Defense as a way of sharing information, even in the event of a war. Due to the built-in redundancy of its communications paths, information could still travel from one computer to another, even if the most direct path between the two were destroyed. Shortly after its development, the research community began to use the Internet to provide access to computers located in remote sites. For example, it was no longer necessary to travel to Boston to use one of the computers at MIT; you could connect to it from any computer that was part of the Internet. In the late 1980s and early 1990s, the Internet's popularity began to grow, and then, in the middle to late 1990s, it began to explode. Nobody knows exactly how many people have access to the Internet, but a study from Nielsen Media Research and CommerceNet puts the North American Internet population at 92 million (Associated Press, June 18, 1999).

As the Internet grew, people developed a variety of useful applications to make it easier to use. Even more significantly, colleges, universities, government agencies, and other organizations made their resources available, usually without charge, to anyone who wanted to use them. In the United States, commercial activity was prohibited on the Internet until the early to mid 1990s; the relaxation of that rule and the development of the World Wide Web (WWW) combined like gasoline and dry grass. These days, just about every company, educational institution, non-profit organization, and government agency has a Website, and Web-based applications are becoming increasingly sophisticated.

This chapter discusses the various ways you can use the Internet to get information, what types of information you might find in your searches, and why the Internet is not always the most reliable or convenient way of getting information. All the examples use Windows 98, Netscape 4.6, and Microsoft Internet Explorer 5.0, but they should apply to other operating systems and newer Web browsers without major changes.

GETTING ACCESS TO THE INTERNET

Chances are that you already have access to the Internet, or you can get access without much difficulty. Almost every college and university is connected to the Internet, and individual accounts are given to students automatically or are free for the asking. Some high schools also provide their students with Internet access. If your school does not provide access, you have other options. In the United States, many public libraries provide Internet access to their patrons. You can also get an account with a commercial Internet Service Provider. There are thousands, and quite possibly tens of thousands, of commercial providers in the United States, Canada, and elsewhere. Fees charged by these providers depend on the kind of service you select. Some providers charge by the hour, some provide unlimited service, and some have other arrangements. Some providers serve only a small area, whereas others, such as America Online and the Microsoft Network, provide service internationally. Some companies will give you a "free" computer if you agree to sign up with an Internet service for a specified time.

TYPES OF INTERNET SERVICE

The most common type of Internet service for home use uses a modem and ordinary telephone line. The speed of the connection is determined by the quality of phone service in your area, the speed of your modem, and the speed of the modem used by your ISP. Typical connection speeds range from 33K (33,000 bits per second, or approximately 3,300 bytes per second) to up to 53K. If your budget runs to more expensive alternatives, some phone companies offer ISDN connections, with a maximum connection speed of 128K, or the latest type of connection, ADSL, which offers connection speeds of over 7MBPS (megabits per second) for downloading and 90K for uploading. Some cable companies also offer Internet service.

BEFORE YOU SIGN UP WITH AN ISP

Here are a few questions to consider before you sign up for Internet service:

What type of service do they offer? Are you getting Web access and one e-mail address? Some ISPs offer separate mailboxes for each member of a family, others give you just one address. Or you might be getting just Web access.

What type of modems do they support? If your ISP only supports modems up to 33K, it doesn't matter how fast a modem you have; you won't be able to transfer data at more than 33K.

How will you connect? If you have to dial a long-distance number to connect, charges will add up quickly. If you travel widely, an ISP with access points throughout the country might be the best option. If you only need access from home, a local company may give you everything you need.

How does the ISP charge for service? If you have to pay by the hour, and you spend fifty hours per month online, an ISP that charges $1.00 per hour with no monthly fee probably isn't as good a choice as one that charges $25.00 per month for unlimited usage. Some companies will offer better rates if you sign (and pay for) a year or more in advance.

How reliable is the ISP? Unlimited Internet access for $9.95 per month isn't much of a bargain if the lines are always busy or their equipment doesn't always work.

WHAT CAN YOU DO ON THE INTERNET?

Although this chapter deals mainly with getting information from the World Wide Web, it should at least mention some of the other things you can use the Internet for.

Electronic Mail. For years, this was the most widely used Internet application, and it is still responsible for a significant portion of Internet traffic. With electronic mail, also known as e-mail, you can send messages to people anywhere on the Internet, usually within a few minutes or even seconds. Most accounts available from commercial ISPs include at least one e-mail address; some include multiple addresses. Some commercial companies, such as Juno, Yahoo!, and Hotmail, will give you a free e-mail address, though getting Internet access to be able to connect to the mail server is your responsibility.

As more sophisticated Internet applications were developed, it became possible to send more complex information via e-mail. Whereas most e-mail systems ten years ago could only handle text, it is now possible to send graphics, sounds, and files created by word-processing programs via e-mail. (This is also a common way for your computer to become infected with a virus. Be sure to use a virus protection program and to keep it activated and updated.)

Discussion Lists (also known as listservs). E-mail provides one-to-one communication; discussion lists provide one-to-many communication. A list is set up to discuss a particular topic, and people subscribe to the list. When a subscriber has something to contribute to the discussion, s/he sends a message to the list server, which is the program that runs the list. (The actual name of the program may be listserv, listproc, majordomo, or one of several other programs. They all do the same thing.) The list server then automatically sends the message to all the subscribers of the list. There are thousands of discussion lists available, with topics ranging from high school physics to Chaucer to disabilities to library technology to vampires.

Usenet. This is not strictly an Internet application, but it is available on many Internet-connected computers. Usenet is a worldwide conferencing system with discussions on almost any topic you can think of, and many that are beyond your wildest imagination. Each newsgroup covers a specific topic, and discussions are expected to stick mainly to that topic. For example, the newsgroup *rec.arts.wobegon* discusses *A Prairie Home Companion* and topics related to the show. Newsgroups have messages, called articles, which users have contributed. Unlike discussion lists, which send messages to each subscriber's mailbox, Usenet stores one copy of each article on the ISP's computer. Users read as many articles as they wish (or have time for), and the articles are deleted from the system after a certain period of time.

Usenet newsgroups are arranged in hierarchies. The main seven, which can be found on most systems, are:

comp	Computer hardware, software, etc.
news	Groups that deal with Usenet administration and announce-ments
rec	Recreation and hobbies
sci	Science
soc	Social and cultural issues
talk	Debates and discussions, usually without end
misc	Topics that don't fit anywhere else

In addition to these seven, two other hierarchies that you might en-counter frequently are:

alt   Alternative topics, often of a bizarre and controversial nature. Generally, users have to vote on whether a new newsgroup is admitted to one of the main seven hierarchies; no such custom exists for the alt groups, so they are easier to create. The alt groups contain much value to people in need of information (the alt.support sub-hierarchy is especially useful to people with health problems and disabilities), but many ISPs and institutions refuse to carry this hierarchy, since much of the pornography available on Usenet can be found in alt newsgroups. (See sidebar on "The Dark Side of the Internet" on pages 53 and 54.)

k12   Topics of interest to elementary and high school students and teachers

There are dozens of other regional, local, institutional, and special-interest newsgroups that are available in certain areas.

Telnet. Telnet lets you connect from your computer to another across the Internet and use it as if you were directly connected to the remote computer. A multitude of library catalogs were once available this way, but now most of them have switched to Web-based catalogs. A slightly different version of telnet, developed by IBM, is known as tn3270.

FTP. FTP, or File Transfer Protocol, lets you connect to a remote computer and copy files from that computer to yours, or from your computer to the remote one. Again, most services once available by FTP are now available via the Web, and most Web browsers will allow you to transfer files via FTP.

IRC and Chat Rooms. Internet Relay Chat (IRC) provides real-time conferencing over the Internet; chat rooms provide the same service in a slightly different manner. IRC and chat rooms can be useful for group discussions, for meeting other people on the Internet, and for communicating with people on other continents. These methods are limited to text only.

Video Conferencing. For less than $100.00, you can buy a small camera that attaches to your computer. Then, using the software that came with the camera or software from a third-party vendor, you can see and talk with people throughout the Internet.

WARNING: All of these Internet applications can be extremely tempting and addictive. It is quite possible to spend hours and hours on the Internet without realizing it, to the detriment of your studies. Fortunately, there are support groups available to help people kick the Internet habit. Unfortunately, many of them are available only on the Internet.

WHAT IS THE WORLD WIDE WEB?

The most popular use of the Internet is the World Wide Web. The basic idea of the Web was developed at the European Particle Physics Laboratory in Switzerland as a way to share information among physicists. Tim Berners-Lee, the developer, used hypertext to create documents that were linked together in ways that would allow readers to move from one document to another as they wished.

In a hypertext document, links are embedded throughout the document to lead readers to more information about the link. For example, a document on the U.S. Congress might have links to the history of the House and Senate, to the Web pages of individual Representatives and Senators, and to articles on the ways lobbyists have influenced the course of legislation in the past 200 years. Each of these links will give you more information on the related topic, and the links themselves may have additional links to related topics.

In the World Wide Web, each link may be on a different computer; a

The Dark Side of the Internet: Pornography, Hate Speech, Predators, and Viruses

The Internet is like a large virtual city, and I would do the reader a great disservice to imply that all parts of it are safe and suitable for all people. Just as it would not be safe to venture into all parts of your hometown, there are certain parts of the Web that are unsafe. None of the problems described below are new, but the wide reach of the Internet has intensified all of them.

Pornography: The invention of the camera made it possible to look at pornographic pictures in the privacy of your home, and the invention of the VCR made it possible to look at pornographic movies in the privacy of your home. It should come as no surprise, then, that the development of the Internet would make it possible to look at a wide variety of pornography in the privacy of your home. A wide variety of Usenet newsgroups are devoted to the distribution of photographs ranging from the mildly naughty to ones that the mere possession of could land you in jail. According to the study cited in the section "Looking for Information on the Web," about 1.5 percent of all Web sites are pornographic. As of this writing, the U.S. Congress and the state legislatures have not come up with a solution that balances free speech and community standards. Some institutions are installing filters to screen out objectionable material. Other laws have proposed limiting the type of information people can make available on Web pages. One problem is that since the Internet is international, restricting what people in the U.S. can make available on the Net will have little effect on what other countries choose to do.

Hate Speech: A similar freedom-of-speech problem as presented by pornography is posed by assorted groups that put up Websites that espouse racism, anti-Semitism, and various other violent causes. Since information can be put up on the Web so easily, it is possible to distribute hate literature far more efficiently and widely than before.

Predators: Is that person you just met in the chat room really someone your own age, or is s/he a convicted sex offender? Remember that advice about not getting into a car with strangers? Sadly, it's true on the Internet, too. Another type of predator is the person who sets up a Web page that looks like it's run by a prosperous business, but is actually just one person taking down credit card numbers. Anyone can set up a Web page, and a sufficiently clever Web designer can make things look like what they are not. In one recent case, someone sent messages to hundreds of customers of a particular ISP, asking them to send in their credit card numbers for verification. The message was sent by someone who had no connection with this ISP.

Viruses: Computer viruses are bits of computer code that attach themselves to other files and make your computer do unexpected things. Some just print strange messages on your screen, but others can alter or destroy data, or even wipe out your entire hard drive. They have been around for years, but until fairly recently, the most common way to spread viruses was by sharing computer disks, or by using a computer that someone else had unwittingly infected when s/he used it. (Incidentally, schools, colleges, universities, and other places that have computer labs used by many people are good places to pick up viruses. A virus can spread through a computer lab as quickly as pinkeye can spread through a daycare center.) New developments in the Internet have made it much easier to spread viruses. For example, e-mail systems that can accept attachments and integrated software packages that can easily open e-mail attachments are especially vulnerable. What could be easier than clicking on an attachment to open it? Unfortunately, if that attachment has a virus, it will spread to your computer. In 1999, a couple of especially malevolent viruses started spreading themselves through the Internet via e-mail. One of them, called the Melissa virus, affected users of Microsoft Outlook. If you used Outlook to look at an e-mail attachment that had the virus, it would send itself to fifty addresses in your Outlook address book using your name. Another virus did much the same thing, but also deleted certain files from your computer's hard drive. In both cases, the person sending the virus was unaware of what was going on. Viruses can also be spread through Websites, though this is still uncommon. As the Internet spreads, and virus writers become more sophisticated, the virus problem will become even more serious. The best way to protect your computer and your work from virus attacks is to use a good virus-scanning program, and to update it frequently.

Wait, Wait, Come Back!: These warnings are not intended to scare you away from the Internet, any more than the chance of meeting bears should keep you away from a hike in the woods. Not every Web page you see will be pornographic, stalkers are not lurking in every chat room, and you will rarely encounter virus-laden Web pages and e-mail messages. If you take appropriate precautions, you shouldn't have any trouble. Don't give out too much information about yourself, don't open an e-mail attachment or run a downloaded program unless you're sure of what it is. Oh yes, and back up your data.

Web page on bird watching in New Jersey may have links to information found on computers in New York, Illinois, Canada, Scotland, and New Zealand that you could use in a term paper on birds.

A FEW ACRONYMS AND OTHER TERMS

As with most computer applications, the Web comes with a host of acronyms and other cryptic terms to contend with. Here are a few of the more common ones:

Client and **Server.** The Web is based on a client/server relationship, in which your computer (the client) sends a request to the computer where the files you want are stored (the server) saying "send me this file." The server sends you the file, and then turns its attention to other clients until you ask it for another file. This is a very efficient way of distributing files, since one server can distribute material to hundreds, or thousands, of clients. The less efficient alternative is a dedicated connection, in which your computer establishes a constant connection to the remote system.

HTML (HyperText Markup Language). Web pages need to have formatting codes to tell the browser what the headlines are, where the graphics should be placed, and where the links go to. These formatting codes form HTML, which is similar to the commands used by typesetting and word-processing programs. A tutorial on HTML is outside the scope of this book, but any bookstore or computer store will have dozens of books and software programs to assist Web page designers. One fast and simple HTML editor is Arachnophilia, available without charge from *www.arachnoid.com*.

HTTP (HyperText Transfer Protocol). This is the method that Web clients and servers use to communicate with each other, and specifying "*http://*" at the beginning of a document that you want to retrieve tells the computer at the other end to communicate via this method. (See URL for more on this topic.)

Page. Each Web document is known as a page. A Web page is similar to one in a book, but it can be of any length and have as many links, graphics, paragraphs, movies, sounds, and paragraphs of text as the designer wants to include. Most Websites have one page that is the starting point of the site. This top page is usually called the homepage.

URL (Uniform Resource Locator). Also known as URI, Uniform Resource Indicator, this is the standard way of referring to an Internet information source. Although it is almost always used to point to Web documents, it can refer to other Internet services as well. A Web URL will have the form "*http://www.organization.domain/ directory/document.html*". The "*http://*" indicates that it is a Web document, the "*www.organization.domain*" is the Internet address of the computer where the document resides, the "*/directory/*" indicates the location within the computer, and "*document.html*" is the file name of the document. (The "*/directory/*" and "*document.html*" parts are not always present, since much of the time you'll be starting with the homepage of an organization. If you use Netscape or Internet Explorer, putting "*http://*" at the beginning of a URL is optional, since both programs will fill it in for you.)

WHAT DO YOU NEED TO ACCESS THE WORLD WIDE WEB?

In order to view Web pages, you will need a Web browser. The first Web browser was Mosaic, which was developed by a team at the National Center for Supercomputing Applications at the University of Illinois at Urbana-Champaign. Most of the team that developed Mosaic then left NCSA to form a company that developed a new Web browser called Netscape. A few years later, Microsoft introduced its own Web browser called Internet Explorer (IE), and the two companies have been battling for supremacy ever since. At the moment, they are about even, with Internet Explorer just slightly ahead in popularity.

Both Web browsers are very easy to obtain. It is quite likely that your ISP has provided you with a browser, and if you are using a computer in a school lab or a library, the computer will almost certainly have a browser already installed. Netscape and IE are available without charge, either from the companies' Websites or on CDs distributed by the millions throughout the country by mail or with other software. Netscape and IE operate in slightly different ways, but they both do basically the same thing: they download Web pages over the Internet and display them on your computer's monitor. The information you retrieve will be the same, but it may be displayed slightly differently. For example, Figure 5–1 shows what the main page of the U.S. House of Representatives looks like in Netscape while Figure 5–2 shows the same page as it displays using Microsoft Internet Explorer.

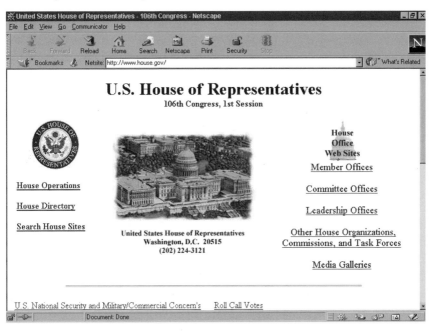

Figure 5–1: The U.S. House of Representatives home page as displayed in Netscape.

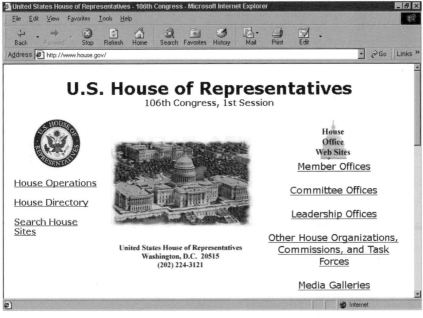

Figure 5–2: The U.S. House of Representatives home page as displayed by Microsoft Internet Explorer.

The first Web browsers were simple and took up only a few mega-bytes on your computer's hard drive. Now, a typical Web browser can play audio and video files, send and receive e-mail, and use a variety of additional programs to provide seamless connections between applications. A typical Web browser also now takes up anywhere from ten to fifty megabytes on your computer's hard drive. Both Netscape and Internet Explorer have far too many features to describe in this chapter, but this chapter covers the basic functions you will need to begin, and how to do them in both Netscape and IE.

CONNECTING TO A SITE

As with most Windows functions, there are several ways to connect to a Web page. Both Netscape and IE have location boxes in which the address of the current page appears. In the above examples, the address is *http://www.house.gov*. To go to a new address, click in the box, delete the current address, type the new one, and hit the *enter* key. Figure 5–3 shows how you would bring up the main page of Yahoo! using Netscape:

Figure 5–3: One way to move from one page to another is to type the new URL into the "Go To" box of your Netscape browser.

Figure 5–4 demonstrates another way to move to another page, which is to click on *File*, then on *Open Page*, which will bring up a box that you can type the new address in. (You can also bring up this box by typing *Ctrl O*.)

Open Page   ☒

Enter the World Wide Web location (URL) or specify the local file you would
like to open:

| yahoo.com | Choose File...

Open location or file in: ○ Composer
                            ● Navigator   Open   Cancel   Help

Figure 5–4: Netscape's "Open Page" command box.

When you hit the *enter* key, the computer tells the remote server that
you want to connect to that particular site, and that you want to download the information on that page. The time that it will take to display
the information depends on how large the files are, and the speed of
the connection between your computer and the remote site. If traffic
on the Internet is very heavy, or if many people are trying to download
the same information, it may take a long time. Both Netscape and IE
will show you how the downloading is going. Figure 5–5 shows an example from Netscape; Figure 5–6 shows the equivalent display using
Internet Explorer.

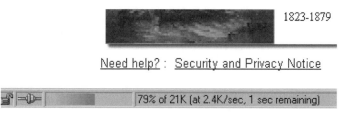

1823-1879

Need help? : Security and Privacy Notice

79% of 21K (at 2.4K/sec, 1 sec remaining)

Figure 5–5: Netscape's transfer speed display, which shows how large a downloaded file is and how much download time remains.

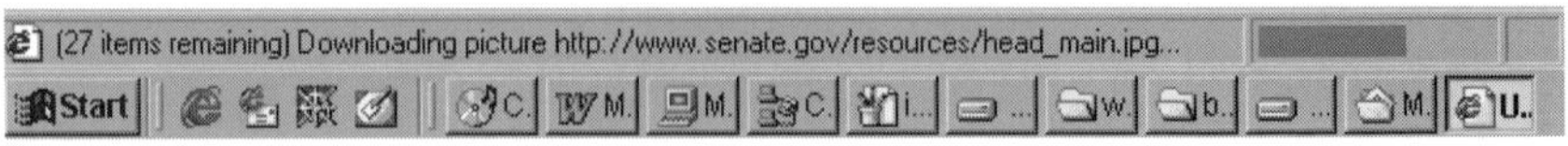

Figure 5–6: MSIE's download transfer display.

If you're tired of waiting, both browsers have *Stop* buttons at the top of the screen.

USING A HYPERTEXT LINK

One of the features of the Web that makes it so easy to use is the ability to link to other documents. Depending on how the Web page is constructed, a link may appear as plain text, or it may appear as an image to click on. In Figures 5–1 and 5–2, the underlined words on either side of the picture (House Operations, House Directory, etc.) are all in blue. If you want to see the House Directory page, click on the words and you will see that page. If you return to the main House page, the link that you have already visited will be displayed in a different color than the links you have not visited. You will also encounter links that are in graphic images. Graphics make pages look better, but at a price, since a graphic-intensive page takes a lot longer to download than a page that is mostly text.

PRINTING A PAGE

Printing a Web page is just like printing anything else in Windows, except for one thing: some Web pages use frames, which divide the screen into parts. If you want to print a page with frames, you need to make sure you're going to print the correct frame. In IE, click the mouse in the frame you want to print, then click on File, Print, and then choose the options from the Print menu (Figure 5–7). In Netscape, click the mouse in the frame you want to print, then click on File, then Print Frame.

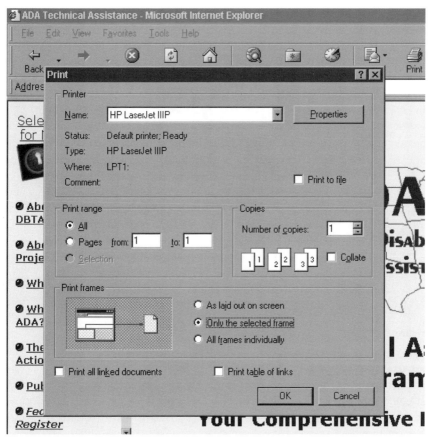

Figure 5–7: MSIE's print control panel.

Netscape allows you to preview a page, so you can see how it will look when you print it: (See Figure 5–8)

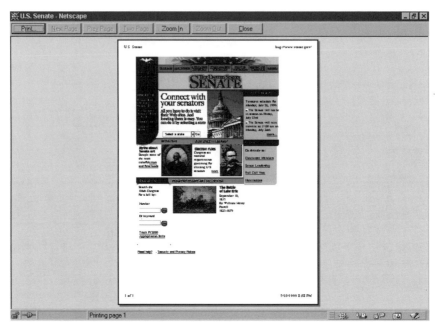

Figure 5–8: Netscape's print preview option.

SAVING IMAGES

If you try saving a Web page, you will end up with a file of HTML codes, text, and links to images. This is fine if you want just the bare text and layout, but if you want to save an image, there's an easier way. Click on the image with the right mouse button to bring up a menu of options (the display in Figure 5–9 uses Netscape; IE works in a similar manner); then choose *Save Image As*, and specify where you want to save the image.

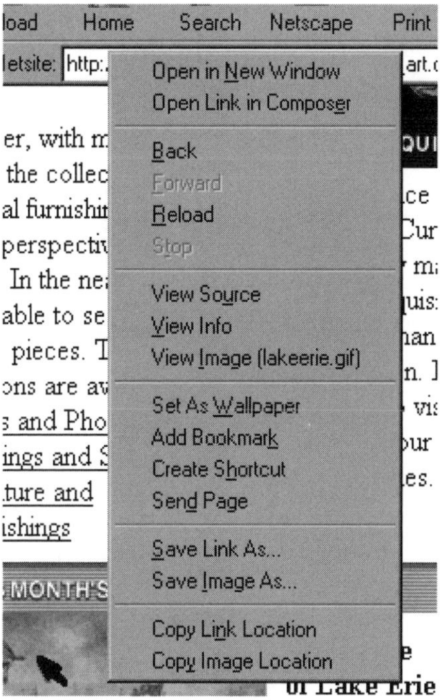

Figure 5–9: Netscape's control panel for saving images, accessed by clicking the right mouse button.

CUT AND PASTE

You can also copy text from a Web page and paste it into another document. This is a great way to enhance research and term papers. This example uses Internet Explorer to copy text from the Library of Congress Copyright Office's Frequently Asked Questions. This is a four-step process:

First (Figure 5–10), highlight the text by holding down the left mouse button and dragging the mouse over the text you want to copy.

Second (Figure 5–11), click *Edit*, then *Copy*.

Third (Figure 5–12), switch to the application you want to paste your selected text into, and click *Edit*, then *Paste*.

Finally (Figure 5–13), check the finished result to make sure it's what you want. In this case, the text has been pasted into Notepad for use as a quote in a paper on copyright.

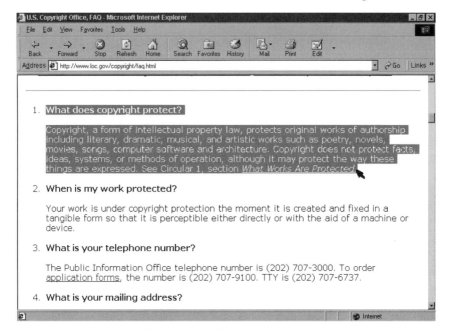

Figure 5–10, Cutting and Pasting, First Step

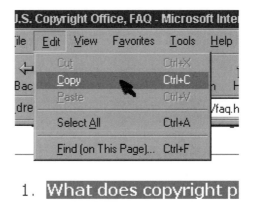

Figure 5–11, Cutting and Pasting, Second Step

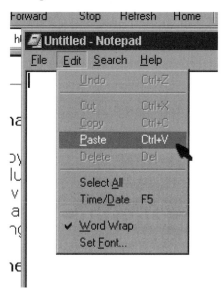

Figure 5–12, Cutting and Pasting, Third Step

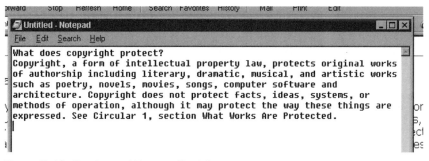

Figure 5–13, Cutting and Pasting, Final Step

I Fear You Have Relied Too Much on Sources*

Plagiarism is nothing new; students (and researchers, scientists, and all types of people in and out of school) have been copying other people's papers, modifying them slightly, and then submitting them as their own work. The main difference is that the Internet makes it a lot easier to cheat. First, there is so much more material available; there are even online collections of term papers on just about any subject available for downloading. Second, if you download something from a Website, you don't even have all that bother of retyping it. Remember, though, that plagiarism constitutes fraud, and can have repercussions beyond receiving a failing grade. If you use someone else's work, remember to document your source, and don't try to claim it as your own.

*An anonymous editor, quoted by Willard R. Espy in *An Almanac of Words at Play* (New York: Clarkson N. Potter, Inc., 1975), p. 216.

BOOKMARKS AND FAVORITES: HOW TO REMEMBER WHERE YOU HAVE BEEN

If you visit a site regularly, or you run across something that is exactly the right source of the information you are looking for, you can write down the address shown in your browser's location bar, or your browser can save the location for you. Netscape calls these saved locations "Bookmarks"; IE refers to them as "Favorites."

Figure 5–14 shows how to save a Netscape Bookmark. First you click on *Bookmarks*, then on *Add Bookmark*.

Then when you want to go to a bookmarked page, click on *Bookmarks*, scroll down to the site you want to visit, and click on the name (See Figure 5–15).

To save an Internet Explorer Favorite, click on *Favorites*, then *Add to Favorites*. IE features a second step, which allows you to customize the name and location of the Favorite. Then when you want to go to a saved Favorite, click on *Favorites*, scroll down to the site you want to visit, and click on the name. If you pause over the name, a window will pop up showing the name and address of the site. Note: If you click on the large Favorites button, all your Favorites will be displayed in a window on the left side of the screen. This makes it easy to get to your favorites, but reduces the size of the Web pages you visit.

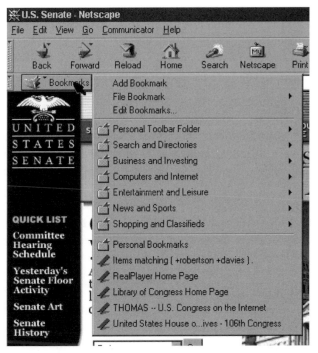

Figure 5–14: Adding the U.S. Senate home page as a bookmark using Netscape.

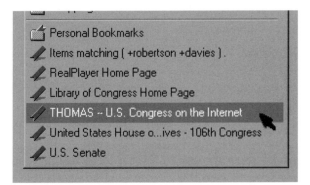

Figure 5–15: Selecting the THOMAS page from Netscape's Bookmark file.

WHAT CAN GO WRONG?

All of these examples have assumed that everything is working perfectly. Anyone who has spent more than a few hours on the Web knows that things do not work perfectly all the time. Here are some of the problems you will encounter as you browse the World Wide Web:

File Not Found. It was there yesterday, but it's gone today. The Web is a very dynamic medium, and things are changing constantly. You may be able to find the file somewhere else, or it may be gone forever.

Remote Server Does Not Respond. The server with the information you need is either overwhelmed by requests from other people, or it is offline entirely. Try again later.

Files Take a Long Time to Download. If you have a slow modem, this will happen a lot. As Web pages get more complicated and graphics-intensive, the files your browser needs to display get larger. Downloading a large file takes time. Also, the remote server may be busy. If your browser seems to be stalled, try clicking the *Reload* button (Netscape) or *Refresh* (IE). If your browser is downloading, but doing it very slowly, the best thing to do is wait. You can learn a lot of things from the World Wide Web. Patience is one of them.

Browser Crashes. If this happens frequently as you try to display different pages, there may be a problem with your browser. Try reinstalling your software. If it happens only with one Web page, there may be a problem with the remote site.

LOOKING FOR INFORMATION ON THE WORLD WIDE WEB

A recent survey by Steve Lawrence and Lee Giles of the NEC Research Institute (*www.wwwmetrics.com*) estimates that the publicly available part of the World Wide Web contains 800 million pages, with six terabytes of text. Approximately 83 percent of Websites have commercial content, 6 percent have scientific or educational content, and 1.5 percent are devoted to pornography. Finding useful information amongst all the advertising can be a bit of a challenge.

Evaluating Web Documents

While you are downloading information from the Internet, you need to remember one very important thing: *Just because you found it on the Internet does not necessarily mean that it is true.*

Anybody with knowledge of HTML can create a Web page, and putting a Web page online usually involves no more than getting an account with an ISP and copying a few files to their server. The most professional and reliable-looking Web page may have nothing behind it but a few bogus statistics.

So how do you tell if the information is reliable? Here are a couple of ways to separate the wheat from the chaff:

Consider the source. Most of the time, it is easy to tell where a Web page comes from. Look at the address in the location bar. If it has an address like *http://users.internetserviceprovider.com/~user/ information.html*, it's probably somebody's personal Web page. (A tilde [~] in front of a username is the way some operating systems configure personal Web pages.) This does not necessarily mean that the information is unreliable, just that it may not be official information from a reliable source.

The Web addresses of U.S. government agencies almost always end in *.gov*. An address such as *www.loc.gov* (in this example, the Library of Congress) generally indicates that the information on the site has been reviewed for accuracy before it was put online.

As someone once noted, the most widely available source of free information is advertising. Some information from commercial companies may not be totally objective, even when they are not recommending a particular product or service. For example, if you are looking for information on the effects of smoking, the information you get from *www.largetobaccocompany.com* will probably be different than information from *www.nih.gov* (the National Institutes of Health) or *www.cdc.gov* (the Center for Disease Control).

And finally, now that it has become very easy to set up one's own Internet domain, some people with particular causes to promote, or axes to grind, can put up official-looking sites that might appear to contain objective information.

When was the document last updated? Even the best sites can go stale quickly. Links to other sites can become outdated, information can be superceded by newer information, and people can leave their jobs and the next person in that position might forget to keep updating the site. If the site is on Medieval English poetry, this might not matter, but if it claims to have the latest news on AIDS treatments, it certainly will. Many sites note the date when the site was last updated; if the information appears to be dated, take it with a grain of salt.

Web Portals and Search Engines

One way to start looking through the Web is by using a Web portal. Portals are sites that provide collections of links to other sites, in an attempt to provide "one stop shopping" for sites. The main pages of portals are usually divided into broad categories, which are then subdivided into narrower categories as you progress through the site. One of the most popular such sites is Yahoo! (*www.yahoo.com*).

Some other recommended sites for searching are:

Northern Light: *www.northernlight.com*
  Special feature: Ranks sites by relevancy.

Snap: *www.snap.com*

AltaVista: *www.altavista.com*
  Special feature: Allows natural language searches (i.e., allows you to state your search in the form of a question).

Hotbot: *www.hotbot.com*

Infoseek: *http://infoseek.go.com*
  Special feature: Ranks sites by relevancy.

Excite: *www.excite.com*
  Special feature: Ranks sites by relevancy.

Lycos: *www.lycos.com*

Dogpile: *www.dogpile.com*
  Special feature: A meta-search site that looks through a variety of search sites, directories, and other Web collections.

Ask Jeeves: *www.askjeeves.com*
  Special feature: A natural-language search site: just type in your

question, and Jeeves will look for the answer. Also has links to numerous search engines.

All of the above are targeted to general audiences, but as the Web continues to grow, some companies are beginning to develop portals geared to specific interests. There will probably come a day when a company will be able to design individual portals based on what you have visited, and what your interests are.

Although each of these search engines indexes only part of the Web, they do not necessarily index the same part of the Web. If you can't find something using one search engine, you might have better luck with another one. Also, there's no guarantee that what you find will actually be relevant to your search: some sites may have totally misleading names, and some sites may be designed to appear relevant to search engines when they are actually not.

Setting Out On Your Own: Information Straight From the Horse's Mouth

After you have gone through all the portals and search engines, there may be times when you still can't find what you are looking for. Or there may be times when you know exactly what you are looking for, and you have a pretty good idea of where you can find it. In that case, you can go directly to the site that has the information. In order to find a site, it helps to know how a Web address is constructed.

THE PARTS OF AN INTERNET ADDRESS

Each computer connected to the Internet has a unique address, so other computers can find it. This address is expressed in a series of numbers; for example, the numeric address of the Library of Congress's homepage is *140.147.248.7*. However, since people remember names better than numbers, many Internet-connected have alphanumeric addresses as well. In the case of the Library of Congress homepage, the address is *www.loc.gov*. These addresses usually have three parts, the domain, the organization name, and the computer name.

Domain. The last part of the address is the domain. In United States Websites, you will likely run into these domains:

.com Commercial companies
.edu Educational institutions

.org Non-profit organizations
.net Network providers
.gov Government agencies
.mil Military branches

Organization Name. The middle part of the address is the name of the organization. The middle section may have more than one name.

netscape.com   Netscape, the developer of a popular Web browser
cua.edu   The Catholic University of America
nlm.nih.gov   The National Library of Medicine at the National Institutes of Health
house.gov   The United States House of Representatives

Computer Name. The first part of the address can be anything the system administrator wants it to be. Most Websites begin with "*www.*" Some sites have just the organization and domain. For example, you can get to Yahoo! by entering "*www.yahoo.com*" or just "*yahoo.com.*"

Outside the United States. Once you venture outside the U.S., most addresses end in a two-letter country code:

.ca Canada
.cl Chile
.ru Russia
.za South Africa
.au Australia
.uk United Kingdom
.us The United States has a two-letter country code as well

Why do you need to know this? For one thing, it makes guessing Web addresses a lot easier. If you don't know the address of an organization, try "*http://www.organization.domain,*" where "*organization*" is the name of the organization, and "*domain*" is the three-letter code for the type of organization it is. This does not always work, and sometimes you can get unexpected results, but it's a good place to start.

Corporate Information

Most commercial companies have Websites with product information, technical support, and other information online. Many mail-order companies will let you place orders online. Try *www.companyname.com.*

Educational Information

The Internet and the World Wide Web have their roots in the educational field, and educational institutions still have a strong presence on the Web. Most colleges and universities have Web pages; many of them have course information, virtual tours of their campus, and instructions on how to apply. If you are choosing a college, this is a good place to start. Many educational institutions put their research projects online as well. Try *www.schoolname.edu.* For example:

> Stanford University: *www.stanford.edu*
> University of Florida: *www.ufl.edu*
> University of Toronto: *www.utoronto.ca* (The University of Toronto is in Canada, so its address ends in *.ca*.)

Organizational Information

If you spend enough time browsing the Web, you may start to think that every non-profit organization in the world has a Website. This probably isn't the case, but there is still a lot of information to be found. Try *www.organization.org.* Here are just a few examples:

> American Heart Association: *www.americanheart.org*
> The Nature Conservancy: *www.tnc.org*
> Public Interest Research Group: *www.pirg.org*

State Information

Most states have Web pages with links to promote tourism, business, education, and other items of interest in their state. Many states have statistical, health, and tax information online as well. Try *www.state.XX.us,* where "*XX*" is the two-letter abbreviation for the state. For example:

> New Mexico: *www.state.nm.us*
> North Carolina: *www.state.nc.us*
> Washington: *www.wa.gov* (If you try *www.state.wa.us,* you will be automatically redirected to the above address.)

U.S. Federal Government Agency Information

Almost every federal government agency has a Web page, and most of them are required by law to make their information available online. If you are looking for environmental information, health information, demographic information, etc., you can probably find it on a U.S. government Web site. Try *www.agencyname.gov*. Here are a few examples:

Environmental Protection Agency: *www.epa.gov*
Resources include environmental research, air-quality statistics, and laws and regulations concerning environmental matters.

Library of Congress: *www.loc.gov*
Access to the Library of Congress catalog, copyright information, online exhibits, and American Memory, a collection of historical photographs and documents.

National Institutes of Health: *www.nih.gov*
Health information, available research grants, and Medline, the National Library of Medicine's database of medical journals.

U.S. Department of Justice: *www.usdoj.gov*
Information on civil rights, community policing, and agencies under the jurisdiction of the Department of Justice.

Internal Revenue Service: *www.irs.gov*
Tax information, including downloadable tax forms.

Census Bureau: *www.census.gov*
All kinds of demographic information, including a gazetteer that allows you to find information by ZIP code.

Fedstats: *www.fedstats.gov*
Links to over one hundred agencies that disseminate statistical information.

U.S. Political Information: How the Government Works

The White House, Senate, and House of Representatives all have Web pages, and several other sites offer information on laws, proposed laws, and other information on the political process.

White House: *www.whitehouse.gov*
Presidential reports, press releases, and an interactive citizen's handbook.

U.S. Senate: *www.senate.gov*
Information on each senator, committees and their jurisdictions, and a calendar of Senate activities.

U.S. House of Representatives: *www.house.gov*
Information on each representative, committee assignments, jurisdictions, and scheduled hearings.

U.S. Supreme Court: *http://supct.law.cornell.edu/supct*
Decisions of the Supreme Court from 1990 to the present. This information is not maintained by the Supreme Court, but rather by the Legal Information Institute at Cornell University.

Thomas: *http://thomas.loc.gov*
A service from the Library of Congress, Thomas has the full text, descriptions, and history of all bills introduced in either the House or Senate from 1989 to the present, and selected information on bills from 1973 to 1989. This site also has a searchable index to the *Congressional Record*, hearing schedules, committee reports, and selected historical documents.

GPO Access: *www.access.gpo.gov*
A service from the Government Printing Office (GPO) that offers the full text of the *Congressional Record, Federal Register, U.S. Code, Code of Federal Regulations,* General Accounting Office reports, the budget of the U.S. government, and much, much more.

KRISTEN AND ZAK SEARCH THE WEB

The first place that Kristen looked was Yahoo! (*www.yahoo.com*), where she typed **television violence** into the search box. Yahoo! had one category devoted to the topic **News and Media > Television > TV Violence** and a total of 22 sites. The most promising appeared to be the National Coalition on TV Violence, but she also found sites on viewer campaigns, children's shows, and a link to the Canadian Broadcast Standards Council (proof, if needed, that TV violence is not solely an American phenomenon).

Kristen then decided to look at some U.S. government sites. The first one she tried was the Federal Communications Commission (*www. fcc.gov*). The search engine on the FCC site found an abundance of press releases, speeches of FCC commissioners, statements from people testifying before the FCC, and public comments. The site was a bit frustrating to use; since the search engine displayed only file names, she had to display the document to find out what it was. After finding out what the FCC had to offer, Kristen then tried the Department of Education (*www.ed.gov*). Their search engine found over 3,000 documents on the Department of Education site, the first 100 of which were sorted by relevance. At the top of the list were ERIC digests (short reports on educational topics produced by the Educational Resources Information Center). Not only did the digests give her a good overview of TV violence, they contained extensive bibliographies for further information. The Department of Education also had fact sheets, radio addresses from the president and vice president, and resource guides for parents and children.

Kristen thought she probably had enough information to start with, but just to be sure, she tried looking at general Web search sites to see what else she could find. Northern Light brought up over 200,000 Web pages, including some additional associations and organizations, pages of links to TV violence, and studies conducted by colleges and universities. She did not look at all the sites offered to her, since it would have taken her several months to do so. Some of the links were no longer valid, and just gave her an error message. (This happens frequently with any search site or list of links, and it can get discouraging, especially when the most interesting links just point to dead ends.) Other search sites did not bring up as many sites. AltaVista found slightly over 4,500, Lycos found 16,000, and Hotbot did not specify how many sites it found. It did, however, have a category on **Television Violence** similar to the one she found on Yahoo! Although Kristen found some overlap in the search engines, there was considerable variety, and even the search engine with the smallest number of sites offered her plenty from which to choose.

Like Kristen, Zak began his search at Yahoo! and found two category matches (**Full Coverage > US > Death Penalty** and **Society and Culture > Crime > Correction and Rehabilitation > Death Penalty**) and 23 sites. Almost all the site matches were in the two categories. Since the categories were both labeled **Death Penalty**, Zak tried searching on that term. **Death Penalty** brought him five categories (of which four were relevant to his topic) and 99 sites. One of the most useful sites he found was the Cornell Law School Death Penalty Project, which had links to Supreme Court cases relevant to the death penalty, and a list of state organizations (including state departments of corrections) that provided information on capital punishment in individual states. Yahoo! also gave Zak links to organizations opposing the death penalty, and to the Usenet newsgroup *alt.activism.death-penalty*.

Next, Zak tried a general search engine. In Northern Light, searching on **death penalty** brought up over 300,000 sites: organizations opposed to capital punishment (such as the American Civil Liberties Union and Amnesty International), sites dealing with criminal law, and much more. A Northern Light search on **capital punishment** produced 100,000 sites.

Zak then wanted to find out what the current U.S. Congress was doing about capital punishment, so he turned to Thomas (*http://thomas. loc.gov*). A search on **death penalty** in the current *Congressional Record* brought up 100 citations. Searching on **capital punishment** produced fewer than 25 articles, most of which Zak had already found in his other search. Zak also looked in current legislation to see what bills on capital punishment were before Congress. Since **capital punishment** is one of the terms that Thomas uses as an example of a subject search, Zak searched on that term; he found 24 citations. (Note: he did this search at the end of the first session of the 106th Congress; if you try this search, your results may vary.)

Finally, Zak looked for death penalty information on a state's Website. On the State of Florida site (*www.state.fl.us*), he found links to the Florida Department of Corrections and the Death Row Fact Sheet. This fact sheet told him how prisoners are executed in Florida, how many prisoners have been executed in Florida since 1976, and described the daily life of a death row inmate. The site also has the full text of any active death warrants. The State of Florida makes provisional copies of state House and Senate bills available, and Zak found several death penalty bills that had been introduced in the current session. To round off his search, Zak looked through Florida statutes to see what the current law was. Zak plans to look at some other states' Websites, but we shall leave him here. His searches illustrate the importance of using more than search terms.

WHAT'S NEXT?

With 800 million Web pages available, it is impossible to do more than just barely scratch the surface of the Web. Although a large percentage of Websites are in North America, the Internet reaches every continent on the globe. Not only would a truly comprehensive Web directory be enormous, it would also be pointless, since the Web changes so quickly. All of the sites mentioned here worked when this chapter was written, but some of them will probably be outdated by the time this book is published. The Web has already brought great changes to the dissemination of information, the entertainment field, and the world of commerce. Although he didn't realize it at the time, Mark Twain gave a very good description of the Web in his book *Life on the Mississippi*, when he described his experience as a steamboat pilot on the Mississippi River:

> Two things seemed pretty apparent to me. One was, that in order to be a pilot a man had to learn more than any one man ought to be allowed to know; and the other was, that he must learn it all over again in a different way every twenty-four hours.

FOR FURTHER READING

Almost any bookstore or computer store will have a large display of Internet- and Web-related books, all of which claim to be the best reference work on the subject. Rather than presenting a list of books that will probably be either out of print or in different editions by the time you read this, here are three publishers whose works are generally informative and well written:

IDG Books: *www.idg.com*
  Well-known for their "For Dummies" series, *www.dummies.com*

Sams Publishing: *www.mcp.com/publishers/sams*
  Fairly technical books on a wide variety of computer-related topics.

O'Reilly & Associates: *www.ora.com*
  Generally more technical than books from IDG or Sams, and a good place to start if you want to delve into advanced HTML, site management, and programming.

Chapter 6

Evaluating Information Sources, Writing, and Revising

Katherine H. Adams and John L. Adams

EXAMINING THE SOURCES

As you continue your research, you should judge the credibility of the authors and the information they present. Facts and opinions from credible sources will make your writing more trustworthy. Consider the following questions when evaluating your sources:

- **The author:** What qualifies the author to speak on the subject? Given the author's credentials and experience, is he or she likely to have a particular bias or be neutral?
- **The source:** Is the publication reputable? Biased? Is it recent or out of date?
- **The audience:** To whom does the author seem to be writing? How does the author deal with the audience's opinions and level of knowledge? Does the author appeal to the readers' emotions?
- **The arguments:** What points does the author try to make?
- **The evidence:** What evidence is offered in support of each point? Is the evidence sufficient?

EVALUATING INTERNET SOURCES

The Internet now provides rapid access to a seemingly infinite amount of information. However, you should take extra care when evaluating

Internet sources. Before a book or journal appears in a library, it has usually gone through a number of checks to make sure the information is reliable. But most sites on the Internet have not been evaluated by publishers, editors, or government agencies. So, in addition to the previous evaluation criteria that apply to a wide range of sources, you should also consider the following questions related specifically to information from the Internet:

- **Who is the author?** Be suspicious of Web pages with no author listed. Also, the information will be more reliable if the author has expertise in the area being discussed, especially if he or she has respected publications in the field of study.
- **Who is the sponsor?** A page can be trusted more if it is sponsored by a reputable person or group, for instance, an academic institution or professional organization.
- **Is contact information provided?** An e-mail address, phone number, or postal address can enhance a source's credibility by providing a way to verify the sponsor's identity.
- **Has the writing also been published elsewhere in printed form?** An article that has been reviewed by a publisher is usually more trustworthy.
- **Can you verify the information you found?** Some pages provide bibliographies or links to more authoritative Web locations. In any case, the data is more valuable for your research if you can check its validity.
- **How well written is the page?** Correct grammar, clear explanations, and logical reasoning can enhance a source's credibility.
- **How well organized is the page?** Although the slickest looking page is not necessarily the most reliable, if the page appears carelessly organized, then its information may have been carelessly compiled.
- **Are there obvious reasons for bias?** Be especially wary of pages sponsored by advocacy groups or by companies promoting a product. Check other sources to determine if the information on such pages has been manipulated unfairly to support a certain view.
- **Is the page current enough?** Like printed texts, Web pages can become too outdated to use for certain topics. Check the dates mentioned in the writing itself and the date when information was last posted. Zombie pages, those still accessible but no longer maintained, usually are not very useful.
- **Is the information primary or secondary?** The further removed

your sources are from the original research, the less reliable the information becomes. For instance, the text of a research study is more credible than comments of a discussion group about the study.

TAKING NOTES

After gathering sources and evaluating their worth, you will be ready to begin taking notes, either on note cards (perhaps the larger 4 × 6 size), in a notebook, or on a computer. The following sections will help you to take notes efficiently.

Write Down the Bibliographic Information

When you begin using a source, first record all the bibliographic information (author, title, publisher, volume, pages, etc.), following the documentation form you will be using in the final draft. (See Chapter 8 for more information on documentation.) Some people use separate bibliography cards or separate pages in their notebooks for these lists.

When taking notes, clearly identify their source. Start each new card or sheet with the title, author's name, or both (if you are using two works by the same author). Then write down the number of the first page you are using and record each additional page number as you proceed so that you will have the complete citations for your paper.

Use a Variety of Note Types

While reading your sources, you may want to take four different kinds of notes—summary, paraphrase, quotation, and personal response—or combinations of them.

Using the computer for note taking

As you conduct your research, you might begin using the computer instead of choosing note cards or a notebook. You can open a separate file for bibliography entries, thus creating a bibliography in almost final form. You could then open another file for your notes, separated by numbers or subheadings for different parts of the paper. If you copy a direct quotation into this file, placing quotation marks around it and noting its source, you will not have to recopy it as you draft and revise.

Summaries. One helpful type of note summarizes the major assertions and evidence of an entire article or chapter, as in the following example from Kristen summarizing "My Pistol Packing Kids," an article by Jean Marzollo on violent play, film, and television:

> Marzollo
> > Watching violence or playing violent games is actually good for children because it allows them to assume some grown-up control, release their frustrations safely, and play together cooperatively.

Paraphrases. Along with summarizing an entire chapter or article, you may want to record the major ideas from individual paragraphs and sentences. Paraphrasing requires you to think carefully about what the author said and then to recast this content *in your own words and sentence structure*. Make sure that you record the page numbers with these notes.

Kristen, for example, decided to paraphrase the following excerpt from the Marzollo article:

> It seems kids want to learn about *both* sides of childhood, not just the mittens and kittens side, full of discovery and nurturing, but also the ghosts and ghouls side, full of dread and helplessness. Watching our children and their friends at play, it is clear to me that the mock violence in their play has a great deal to do with their need to *do* something about the underside of their lives. In order to fight back the witches, giants, and werewolves that menace them at night, they run around in the daytime with toy pistols, toy knives, and toy swords. When I stop to think about their play in these terms, I find I can accept it (607).

Here is Kristen's paraphrase:

> Marzollo
> Page 607. Children want to understand the dark and dangerous side of life as well as the innocence of childhood. Violent, imaginative play helps them feel, if only temporarily, as though they can control the larger forces that they don't really understand.

Quotations. You may decide to quote some memorable phrases or sentences directly. (See pp. 87–89 for help with deciding when to use a direct quotation.) Write down every word exactly, mark the quotation with quotation marks so that later you will not mistake it for a paraphrase, and record the page numbers. At this point, you might also make a note about how you could use the quotation in your paper:

> Marzollo
> Page 607: Violent play comes from children's "need to *do* something about the underside of their lives," about "the ghosts and ghouls side, full of dread and helplessness." These lines are good for stating a common attitude about outside play that this parent also applies to television and movies.

Personal Responses. As you read source materials, you will be changing your own view of the topic. Use a separate card or sheet and write "ME" on it to separate the notes that record your own thinking from summaries, paraphrases, and quotations. Do not wait until later or the idea may be gone.

> Marzollo
> ME: She bases her argument just on her children and they're both boys—not much real research here. She wants to believe that this violence is all right, a trait she shares with many parents.
> For the introduction—playing rowdy games outside is different from television but many parents don't want to acknowledge the difference.

CHOOSING A PRELIMINARY THESIS AND OUTLINE

When you have investigated your topic thoroughly, you will be ready to organize a paper by choosing a thesis and outline.

Deciding on a Tentative Thesis

A *thesis* is a sentence that presents the main idea of the paper, an idea that every fact and detail should support. Although you may alter it after you write a first draft, formulating a thesis now will help you to organize your ideas.

A good thesis has these qualities:

- It states the paper's topic.

- It states a specific opinion or attitude concerning that topic.
- It informs and interests your readers.

When Kristen finished her research on parents' attitudes toward television violence, she realized that she needed a strong thesis to get their attention and state her viewpoint. She first wrote the following sentence:

Playing cops and robbers games may not be harmful to children, but watching violent television can be.

Kristen then decided on this revision to express her opinions more specifically:

Playing cops and robbers games may not be harmful to children, but watching violent television each day can make them aggressive, afraid, and less capable of complex thinking.

As Zak investigated thoroughly, he decided that he would argue against capital punishment to his audience of fellow students, who had shown overwhelming support for it in his survey. He wrote the following thesis to state his topic and his opinion concerning it and to address his readers' beliefs:

Although capital punishment may seem like a fair manner of securing justice, it should be abandoned because it is instead a form of prejudice against the poor of a few states, it doesn't deter crime, and its costs are the highest of any punishment option.

Deciding on a Tentative Outline

After choosing a thesis statement, you should reread your research notes and group them into subtopics. You will then be ready to create a preliminary organization, which may be altered as you write and revise. One structure frequently used for presenting research data is thesis/support:

Introduction
    Background Information
    Thesis Statement

    1. Consideration of the Audience's Beliefs on the Issue
    2. *Your First Main Point* (beginning the proof of your thesis)

3. *Your Second Main Point* (building on the first point and continuing the proof of the thesis)
4. *Your Third Main Point* (building on the first and second points and continuing the proof of the thesis)
   (Continuing with additional points)

Conclusion
  Restatement of the Thesis
  Address to the Reader
  Statement of Implications or a Call to Action

This structure allows you to address any common misunderstandings about the issue and then move into your own arguments concerning it. Another possibility is to refute other viewpoints as you present your own.

Zak decided to begin with his audience's desire for a punishment to equal the crime, which they had indicated on their survey. He decided to then begin his own arguments against the death penalty:

Introduction
  Background Information. Survey data on the readers' attitudes on capital punishment.
  Thesis Statement. Although capital punishment may seem like a fair manner of securing justice, it should be abandoned because it is instead a form of prejudice against the poor of a few states, it doesn't deter crime, and its costs are the highest of any punishment option.

1. *Consideration of the Audience's Beliefs on the Issue.* The desire for justice, which I have shared, is a natural one, but no system can offer a punishment to really equal the crimes.
2. *Your First Main Point.* About the poor of a few states: Only poor and minorities, primarily in a few southern states, currently await capital punishment.
3. *Your Second Main Point.* About deterrence: Capital punishment does not stop crimes from occurring.
4. *Your Third Main Point.* About cost: Capital punishment is the most expensive form of punishment.

Conclusion Capital punishment should be abolished nationally.

WRITING THE FIRST DRAFT

Before you start work on a first draft, place your research materials in an order that reflects your outline so that you can find the relevant information easily.

When you begin to write, however, don't feel restricted by this planning. If new ideas come to mind that don't seem to fit with your thesis and outline, write them down anyway to insure that you do not forget them. In fact, you should try to get down every point that may persuade your readers and explain your opinions; you can restructure to incorporate these ideas as you revise. And don't worry about spelling and grammar: they will come later.

Kristen decided when she made her outline to first address her audience's comparison of play and television and then develop her own points on violent behavior, fear, and poor thinking skills. Here is the draft of her second paragraph:

> The effect of television on children has been under investigation for the past few decades. Hundreds of studies and experiments have been conducted which support the theory that television violence has a significant effect on the aggressive tendencies of children. Joe Frost says that as early as 1973 "studies were showing that watching television led to aggressive behavior" (5). Lilian Katz states in one article, "children simply mimic the behavior they observe" (113). One study, involving children who were shown soap operas, reported that the usual game of "mommy and daddy" quickly changed into "you get pregnant, you run away, and you get shot" (Davidson and Pliska 6). This example demonstrates how impressionable young children can be. Another study, conducted for eleven days on preschoolers, had similar results. They viewed several violent cartoons; soon after, a sharp increase of aggression during play was recorded, such as kicking, choking, hitting, and pushing. Most aggressive acts were similar to those from the cartoons (Davidson and Pliska 6).

After she finished, Kristen realized that she had stated her topic and provided data, but she needed to clarify the relation between the studies and her topic.

WORKING WITH SOURCES

As you write your first draft and later as you revise, you will be working on effective and correct use of your sources in direct quotations, paraphrases, and summaries. Using your notes, you can collect and shape the materials that will support your arguments and convince your readers.

Quoting Sources Effectively

As you work on a first draft, you will need to decide when to quote directly and when to paraphrase your research sources. The key to quoting is not to overdo it. With too many quotations, certainly over two or three on a page, the writing will be choppy, the argument will be unclear, and your own voice will be buried by the others.

You should choose a direct quotation in only two circumstances:

- when you want to provide a sample of a writing style or dialect
- when a point or policy is particularly well stated and the exact words are important to your argument

In the following excerpt on marketing violent television shows, for example, the children's speaking style helps us understand their logic:

> Even though most of the children I interviewed at the video arcade were terribly naive about money and the capitalist system, they seemed keenly aware of the dynamics of consumerist desire. They knew from their own experience that the reported popularity of a commodity and its promotion through commercial tie-ins greatly intensify its desirability to consumers. For example, when asked why they thought Teenage Mutant Ninja Turtles were so popular, one 8-year-old Caucasian boy responded, "Because everybody knows about them and they have lots of stuff," and a 10-year-old Latino boy replied, "They are selling a lot of stuff in stores and usually I buy things like that." (Marsha Kinder, *Playing with Power: In Movies, Television, and Video Games* 123)

In this second excerpt from the same source, the direct quotation is used to clearly state a company's goals and indicate the attitudes of the spokesman:

The producers of the original TMNT [Teenage Mutant Ninja Turtle] movie took the young core audience for granted and tried to appeal as well to parents and teens (who were probably the readers of the original comic book)—and so they went for a PG rating rather than a G. As Tom Gray, the Los Angeles-based executive in charge of the production company, Golden Harvest, claimed before the film's release: "We purposely skewed this movie for an *older* audience. We know that the kids would come, but we really wanted to make it for the teenage and university level. The script is very, very hip and very timely. We will probably end up with a PG-13 or a PG. . . . A G-rating would kill us." (Kinder 132–33)

Choosing Short Quotations. When you have decided that a quotation will be effective because it meets one of these two criteria, choose as short an excerpt as possible to keep the quoted material from overwhelming your own developing argument.

Zak, for example, might want to discuss contradictory attitudes about capital punishment by quoting from this part of Anna Quindlen's essay on her personal responses to mass murderer Ted Bundy:

In a rational, completely cerebral way, I think the killing of one human being as punishment for the killing of another makes no sense and is inherently immoral.

But whenever my response to an important subject is rational and completely cerebral, I know there is something wrong with it—and so it is here. I have always been governed by my gut, and my gut says I am hypocritical about the death penalty. That is, I do not in theory think that Ted Bundy, or others like him, should be put to death. But if my daughter had been the one clubbed to death as she slept in a Tallahassee sorority house, I would with the greatest pleasure kill him myself.

The State of Florida will not permit the parents of Bundy's victims to do that, and, in a way, that is the problem with an emotional response to capital punishment. (Anna Quindlen, "Death Penalty's False Promise: An Eye for an Eye" pp. 138–39)

Instead of using the entire excerpt, he should quote only the part that is essential to his argument and then continue with his own writing, as in these examples employing MLA documentation (See pp. 111–120):

Many people, like author Anna Quindlen, find "the killing of one human being as punishment for the killing of another" to be "inherently immoral" (138).

Quindlen contrasts her "rational, completely cerebral" opposition to capital punishment with her realization that if her own child were the victim of a brutal murderer, "I would with the greatest pleasure kill him myself" (138–39).

Using Ellipses and Brackets with Quotations. By using the ellipsis mark (. . .), you can eliminate part of a quoted sentence and thus produce a shorter quotation that highlights the information essential to your argument. Make sure, though, that the alteration does not distort the meaning of the original work. If some words need to be changed so the quotation will fit into your sentence structure or if you need to add information to clarify the meaning, you can make those small changes within brackets ([]).

If Zak quoted from the Quindlen essay, for example, he might want to shorten the final sentence from the excerpt above:

Even though she opposes the death penalty, author Anna Quindlen does not criticize a family member's desire for revenge against the murderer: "But if my daughter had been the one clubbed to death . . . , I would with the greatest pleasure kill him myself" (139).

He might need brackets if he quoted only the final sentence from the excerpt by itself:

Although capital punishment may seem to offer justice, families often find that it does not fulfill their personal desire for vengeance: "The State of Florida will not permit the parents of Bundy's victims to do that [kill him themselves], and, in a way, that is the problem with an emotional response to capital punishment" (Quindlen 139).

Punctuating Quotations. As the above examples show, *quoted phrases or words* can be incorporated into your sentences within quotation marks. No additional punctuation is required.

Voters must move beyond "an emotional response to capital punishment" and instead rationally consider the facts about deterrence and cost.

When the quotation will be followed in your sentence by a comma or period, place it within the quotation marks:

> Quindlen recognizes that her opinions have been altered by her "three years as a mother," and she admits that any victim's parent might want "something as horrifying as what happened to his child to happen to Ted Bundy."

When you use a *quoted sentence,* join it to the preceding sentence with a colon:

> Anna Quindlen clearly states her reasoned objection to capital punishment: "In a rational, completely cerebral way, I think the killing of one human being as punishment for the killing of another makes no sense and is inherently immoral."

When MLA parenthetical documentation is used at the end of a sentence, the page numbers placed in parentheses come before the period:

> Quindlen believes that capital punishment is not a deterrent to crime because the criminals she has met have "sneered at the justice system" (139).

When you use a longer quotation, one that is more than four lines, indent it ten spaces from the left margin. The quotation should be double spaced, with double spacing also between the quotation and your text. Do not use quotation marks. The MLA documentation should appear outside of the final period:

> Quindlen writes about criminals she has interviewed to explain why capital punishment doesn't deter crime:
>> The ones I have met in the course of my professional duties have either sneered at the justice system, where they can exchange one charge for another with more ease than they could return a shirt to a clothing store, or they have simply believed that it is the other guy who will get caught, get convicted, get the stiffest sentence. (139)

Paraphrasing and Summarizing Sources

Since you should choose the direct quotation in only the two situations mentioned above, you will generally use a paraphrase or summary when you discuss ideas and facts from sources.

To summarize or paraphrase, you put the author's ideas *completely into your own words* instead of creating some odd combination of the text's original wording and your own. Consider, for example, this excerpt from an essay on the impact of television and film violence that Kristen wanted to use to support her arguments:

> In panel discussions on this subject, we usually hear claims from TV and movie industry spokespersons that opinion is divided in the medical community. Different conclusions can be drawn from different studies, so the arguments go, and no clear consensus exists. Yet, the American medical establishment is clear—in print—on the subject of just such a consensus. The American Medical Association, the National Institute of Mental Health, the U.S. Surgeon General's Office, the U.S. Centers for Disease Control and the American Psychological Association have concluded that study after study shows a direct causal link between screen violence and violent criminal behavior. (David S. Barry, "Growing Up Violent," p. 125)

If Kristen decided to paraphrase the first sentence of this excerpt, she would need to put it into her own words:

> *Inadequate paraphrase*: In panel discussions on television violence, media spokespersons usually claim that the medical community is divided in its opinion of the topic (125).

> *Adequate paraphrase*: Television and film representatives refuse to admit that medical researchers have identified harmful effects from repeated viewing of violent shows (125).

A good method of paraphrasing is to read the source material, put it down, think through the information, and then write your own version of it.

Introducing Quotations, Paraphrases, and Summaries

One method of introducing the quotation or paraphrase is with a *signal phrase*, which explains to the reader the author's authority or intentions and thus makes the excerpt more meaningful:

> Anna Quindlen, a liberal columnist who has opposed capital punishment, admits that "my gut says I am hypocritical about the death penalty" (139).

David S. Barry, in an article published by the Center for Media and Values, argues that "study after study shows a direct causal link between screen violence and violent criminal behavior" (125).

When you want the subject matter to remain central, you can also use the *dropped-in quotation or paraphrase*, for which the author's name is supplied in the parenthetical documnentation:

Many medical organizations, such as the American Medical Association and the Centers for Disease Control, have concluded that television violence causes harm to viewers (Barry 125).

Verb Choices for Introducing Quotations, Paraphrases, and Summaries

When you use a signal phrase to introduce source materials, you might want to choose a more specific verb than *said* to indicate the author's attitude or approach. The following verbs create different meanings that may better represent an author's intentions:

admits	notes
agrees	observes
analyzes	opposes
claims	points out
comments	predicts
concludes	proposes
condemns	relates
considers	reports
describes	sees
disagrees	shows
explains	suggests
insists	thinks
maintains	warns

Avoiding Plagiarism

As you present source materials—quotations, paraphrases, or summaries—you will need to provide documentation for them.

Citations give appropriate credit to the author and enable your readers to locate relevant materials. Correct documentation requires that all direct quotations, placed in quotation marks, be the author's exact words and that all paraphrases be completely in your own words and sentence structure.

The only exception to the requirement to cite all source materials occurs when you decide that a certain fact is "common knowledge" in the field you are researching. Examples would include the dates of a war or weight of a molecule. If you are in doubt about whether to give credit, however, go ahead and cite the source: no teacher will fault you for being overly careful.

Failing to cite a source, either intentionally or unintentionally, is called *plagiarism* (from the Latin word for "kidnapper"). It is a form of stealing, and thus a punishable offense, since it involves pretending that another person's work is your own.

REVISING

When you have finished a rough draft that incorporates your source materials, your next step is to begin revising, which means "re-seeing" your work from big to small, starting with the thesis and overall structure and then moving to each paragraph and each sentence—to create the best paper that you can.

To begin this step, read your paper carefully and consider the following questions:

1. **Introduction:** Does the beginning involve the reader? Does it state the needed background material?
2. **Thesis:** What is the thesis of the essay? Does it seem clear? Does the body of the paper prove this assertion?
3. **Structure:** Make an outline of the paper's contents. Does the order of points seem appropriate? Should any point be added, moved, or deleted?
4. **Evidence:** Does the essay contain sufficient supporting detail?
5. **Use of source materials:** Are the direct quotations and paraphrases woven into the paper? Are there any direct quotations that might be removed or shortened? Are all paraphrases correctly done? Are all source materials documented?
6. **Conclusion:** Are the implications of the argument made clear? Is there a call to action or further discussion of the argument's importance?

As Kristen reread her draft, she decided that her thesis was clear and that the structure enabled her to develop each part of her thesis. She had devoted one paragraph to each of her claims: that watching violent television each day makes children aggressive, isolated, and less capable of complex thinking. Within her body paragraphs, however, Kristen realized that she needed better evidence and citation.

As she worked on the second paragraph (for which the first draft is provided on p. 86), she decided that she needed a stronger topic sentence, to clearly develop part of her thesis. (A tightened version of her second sentence became that topic sentence.) She also needed to add a more recent expert opinion, identify the authorities more clearly, and include more specific explanations of the research studies that would indicate their relationship to her argument. And she decided to move the material on soap operas to the next paragraph since it related to fear instead of aggression. Her revised essay is found on pp. 98–103.

When Zak reread his draft, he was pleased with his thesis and overall structure. He decided to work further on developing his paragraphs, especially his conclusion where he decided to do more than just repeat his criticism of capital punishment and instead discuss moral issues and advocate sentences of life in prison. (His revised essay appears on pp. 104–110.)

Chapter 7

Proofreading and Preparing the Final Copy

Katherine H. Adams and John L. Adams

PROOFREADING

After you finish revising, you will be ready to proofread your paper. At this point, you will need to quit thinking about the ideas and focus on the grammatical correctness of each sentence and the spelling of each word, a task that is easier if you take a break before you begin and allot enough time, perhaps five minutes for each paragraph. Try the following techniques to then turn yourself from writer and reviser into proofreader.

Reading Out Loud

If you read silently, you may think words are there that are not because you will be remembering what you meant to say. Reading the material out loud slowly will help you to focus on what is really there, on each word, and on each mark of punctuation.

Reading Paragraphs Out of Order

Another helpful technique is to read paragraphs out of order: perhaps the third and then the second or the fifth paragraph. This method will force you to look carefully at the actual words and sentences. You might place a ruler or pencil below each sentence to stop you from reading and thinking ahead.

Using Computerized Spelling and Grammar Checkers

You may also find it helpful to use computerized spelling checkers, but you need to recognize their limitations as well as their strengths.

Instead of noticing all errors, the spelling checker actually points out words that are not in its dictionary. If the computer tells you that a proper noun is "misspelled," it may be correct but missing from the dictionary. Since the spelling checker only tells you whether a word is in its dictionary, it cannot determine whether you have used the wrong word, such as "affect" for "effect" or "there" for "their." After you use a spelling checker, you should proofread for this type of error.

You can check your grammar by using a computerized grammar or style checker. These programs isolate spelling errors, grammatical errors, and poor stylistic choices like passive constructions and overly long sentences. Some also offer explanations of grammar rules.

Like spelling checkers, however, grammar programs have limitations. Even if you agree with the program's analysis of the error, perhaps in subject-verb agreement, you may want to choose another method of correcting it: the checker may suggest changing a subject and predicate verb to the singular, for example, when you meant for them to be plural. Since these checkers do not locate all errors, you will still need to review your sentences carefully.

PRODUCING THE FINAL COPY

When you are ready to produce the final copy, follow these MLA guidelines:

1. Set one-inch margins on the top, bottom, and sides of each page.
2. Number each page, in the upper right corner, one inch from the right and one-half inch from the top. Type your last name before the number. On a word processor, your name and the page number can be placed in the header.
3. You do not need a title page. On the first page of the paper, type your name, your instructor's name, the course number, and the date on separate lines beginning at the left margin one inch from the top. Double-space between each line. Then double-space again and type the title—centered—without underlining it or placing it in quotation marks. Then double-space again and begin typing the text.
4. Indent the first word of each paragraph 5 spaces from the left; indent block quotations 10 spaces.

5. Double-space the entire text, including indented quotations and the list of works cited.

6. Use a separate page, at the end of the paper, for your references. Center the words "Works Cited" at the top of the page. Type the first line of each entry at the left margin; each subsequent line should be indented five spaces. Double-space within and between all entries.

SAMPLE ESSAYS

Kristen and Zak's finished, proofread, and polished final papers are presented in the appendix for you to use as models. We've made comments where they have used especially important writing techniques presented earlier in this book.

APPENDIX

Model Paper I

Kristen Hubbard
Dr. Lawrence
English 101
April 17, 1999

Television Violence and Our Children

Children have always made forts and played war games, without much negative effect on their behavior toward parents or friends. These games, in fact, may enable them to assume some grown-up control, release their frustrations safely, and play together cooperatively (Marzollo). Many parents seem to believe that watching violence on television is similar to harmless "shoot-em-up" games. But parents need to realize, however, that the games of their youth are very different from the television experience of today. Young people watch television an average of 16 to 17 hours each week, viewing approximately 10,000 acts of violence per year (Strasburger & Donnerstein). Although playing cops and robbers games may not be harmful to children, watching this amount of violent television can make them aggressive, afraid, and less capable of complex thinking. **(1)**

---

1. Kristen begins by addressing her readers' beliefs and then moves to her thesis. In this paragraph, she summarizes opinions and data with dropped-in paraphrases.

Hundreds of studies and experiments support the conclusion that television violence has a significant effect on the aggressive tendencies of children. As parents, we expect them to mimic many behaviors, such as our manners at a party or treatment of a pet. They will also mimic what they see on a machine they sit in front during the afternoons and evenings and throughout the weekends (Katz 113). As American Medical Association Trustee John C. Nelson recently claimed, physicians and health care officials are concerned about television violence because "[t]here is a profound and causal relationship between repetitive viewing of violence and what children do" (qtd. in Stapleton). Joe Frost, a British psychologist, contends that as early as 1973, "studies were showing that watching television led to aggressive behavior" (5). In one such study, preschool children played together, viewed several violent cartoons, and then played again. In the second play sessions, researchers noted a sharp increase in aggressive acts, such as kicking, choking, hitting, and pushing, that were similar to those from the cartoons (Davidson and Pliska 6). Another study of preschoolers judged the postviewing behavior of boys who watched live television programs with violent content and then played with toys that encouraged aggressive behavior. On that day and during the next few weeks, they used the toys to make verbal and physical attacks that mimicked the

shows' action (Pots, Hutson, and Wright 13–14). All of these studies leave little doubt that children imitate what they see. **(2)**

Violence on television also affects children's perception of the
actual violence in their environment and thus makes them afraid. In
one study of children watching soap operas, the usual game of
"mommy and daddy" quickly changed into an imitation of soap op-
era plots, including "you get shot" (Davidson and Pliska 6). These
children feared violent attacks on their own families. According to
Erin Broussard, child psychologist and expert on television, children
exposed to local news often fear that robbers or murderers will
enter their homes. Police dramas give them the impression that children are likely to be kidnapped or hurt when a crime is commit-
ted. Cartoon violence reinforces the notion that physical attacks are
inevitable and acceptable. All three types of shows can lead to feel-
ings of isolation and fear and thus to lowered self-confidence. **(3)**

Today's violent shows, with their quick cuts and multiple plot
lines, also affect children's abilities to make connections between
causes and effects, to understand real human behaviors. The speed
of violence, found in videos, drama, cartoons, and the news, thus
cripples the child's ability to think logically about crisis events. This
"scattered, fragmented form" trivializes the meaning of each occur-

---

2. Kristen uses the tag and quotation to present Frost's findings.
3. This paragraph includes information from Kristen's interview.

rence (Bogart 255). As Neil Postman contended in his ground-breaking piece "Future Schlock," television viewers become used to seeing any type of violence, such as that perpetuated in Hitler's concentration camps, as entertainment and have no interest in a detailed analysis of the reality. Observations of the cartoon viewing of my own brothers, ages five and seven confirmed these findings. As they watched *Power Rangers* and similar actions shows, every scene seemed entertaining to them, and they especially seemed to enjoy the kicking fights, which they reenacted as they watched. When I asked them why the cartoon heroes were being pursued and attacked, how they could escape, and what they could do to avoid a repeat attack, my brothers had no answers. They were simply taking in quick scenes as they occurred without having the time, or perhaps the ability, for reflection. **(4)**

David S. Barry, in an article published by the Center for Media and Values, argues that "study after study shows a direct causal link between screen violence and violent criminal behavior" (125). He cites research done by the American Medical Association, the U.S. Surgeon General's Office, and the U.S. Centers for Disease Control to prove this assertion. We need to heed these warnings and refuse to surrender our children to that box in the den. Lim-

---

4. Her observations and discussions with her brothers provided her data here.

ited viewing, no more than an hour a day, may be harmless, but children should not be allowed to spend their evenings and weekends plugged into the set. We cannot wait for federal legislation, but instead we must take action ourselves. Just as you might keep your children from eating only candy or walking down an interstate, you should drag them away from the set. **(5)**

Works Cited

Barry, David S. "Media's Violence Contributes to Society's Violence." *Mass Media: Opposing Viewpoints*. Ed. William Barbour. San Diego: Greenhaven, 1994. 123–28.

Bogart, Leo. "Advertising Perpetuates Consumerism." *Mass Media: Opposing Viewpoints*. Ed. William Barbour. San Diego: Greenhaven, 1994. 250–55.

Broussard, Erin. Personal Interview. 11 Feb. 1995.

Davidson, Sunny, and Mary Pliska. *Parents Guide for Non-Violent Toy-Buying*. Washington, D.C.: United Methodist Church Board of Society, 1986.

Frost, Joe L. "Influences of Television on Children's Behavior: Implications for War and Peace." International Association for the Child's Right to Play Seminar. London, 29 Dec. 1986. ERIC ED 103 922.

---

5. Kristen ends with a strong address to her readers.

Katz, Lilian G. "As They Grow—3 and 4: How TV Violence Affects Kids," *Parents* Jan. 1991: 113.

Marzollo, Jean. "My Pistol Packing Kids." *The Macmillan Reader.* Ed. Judith Nagell, John Langan, and Linda McMeniman. 3rd ed. New York: Macmillan, 1993. 605–12.

Postman, Neil. "Future Schlock." *The Macmillan Reader.* Ed. Judith Nagell, John Langan, and Linda McMeniman. 3rd ed. New York: Macmillan, 1993. 247–60.

Pots, Richard, Aletha C. Huston, and John C. Wright. "The Effect of Television Form and Violent Content on Boys' Attention and Social Behavior." *Journal of Experimental Child Psychology* 41(1986): 1–17.

Stapleton, Stephanie. "TV Watchers Want Content Info." *American Medical News* 40.11 (1997). 22 February 1999 <*http//web3. searchbank.com/itw/session/141/22/29345951w3/11!xm_3_0_A19228390*>.

Strasburger, Victor C., and Edward Donnerstein. "Children, Adolescents and the Media: Issues and Solutions." *Pediatrics* 03 (1999). 22 February 1999 <*http://gilligan.prod.oclc.org:3057/FETCH:. . . . :next=netml/fs/ fulltext.htm%ww:fstxt4.htm*>.

Model Paper II

Zak Cernok
Dr. Amato
English 1104
October 12, 1998

A Call for Abolition

At my school, the majority of students, like the majority of
Americans, seem to favor capital punishment. A recent survey I conducted indicated that 79 percent of 105 male and female students
viewed the death penalty as appropriate for murderers, of one person or of several. A much lower number, under 10 percent, viewed
it as appropriate for any other crime. The students' main reason
for supporting capital punishment in murder cases was that it offered a penalty equal to the crime. As one student stated, "These
killers should get what they dished out." Seventy-five percent also
believed that capital punishment was being fairly administered across
the nation to combat crime. I agreed with these opinions until I stud-
ied the issue more carefully. I now believe that although capital punishment may seem like a fair manner of securing justice, it should
be abandoned because it is instead a form of prejudice against the
poor of a few states, it doesn't deter crime, and its costs are the
highest of any punishment option. **(1)**

---

1. Zak begins with his survey to present the misconceptions he will
   refute.

Capital punishment might seem like an appropriate penalty if it allowed victims to exact a punishment equal to the crime. Anna Quindlen, a columnist who opposes the death penalty, admits that any victim's parent might want "something as horrifying as what happened to his child to happen to Ted Bundy," a mass murderer captured after attacking women students at Florida State University (140). But this desire is not fulfilled by the death penalty. A mass murderer does not endure an equally hideous experience by sitting in the chair and receiving a quick, painless injection. His years living in a clean and safe cell attended by lawyers and physicians certainly do not equal what his victims experienced. Since the desire for vengeance cannot actually be served by the justice system, this personal need is not an adequate defense for a punishment that every other Western industrialized nation has abandoned (Zimring 3). **(2)**

Since capital punishment is not dispensing the personal style of justice we seek, we must look at what its purposes and effects really are. Race, economic status, education, and state of prosecution have been the most dominant factors in determining who will or will not be executed in the United States. According to Missouri Congressman William L. Clay, Sr., "few 'rich' persons, if any, have

_____

2. The quotation from Quindlen states the attitude Zak will discuss in this paragraph.

ever gone to the gallows. The ranks of the condemned are heavily populated by poor whites—those condemned for reasons other than their specific crimes—and by minorities who are damned by socio-economic pressures" (7). Former governor of California Edmund (Pat) Brown points out that "dozens of reputable studies show that the race of the victim as well as that of the criminal plays a vital part in deciding whether a murderer lives or dies" (160). A 1980 survey by William Bowers and Glenn Pierce concluded that, in Georgia, blacks who killed whites were 84 times more likely to receive the death penalty than blacks who killed blacks; in Texas, blacks who killed whites were 84 times more likely to receive death sentences. The study also found that killers of black victims, whether they were white or black themselves, were punished by death less than one-tenth as often as killers of white victims. Another study found that "there has been a systematic, differential practice of imposing the death penalty on blacks and, most particularly, when the defendants are black and their victims are white" (Zimring 35). And a 1998 U.N. Report criticized the U.S. for its "unfair, arbitrary, and racist" use of the death penalty (Olson). These prejudicial decisions also occur in only a few states. From 1972 to 1996, of 358 executions, 227 occurred in Texas, Florida, Louisiana, Georgia, and Virginia (*Statistical Abstract*, Table 383). **(3)**

---

3. Data from a Congressman, governor, researchers, and the *Statistical Abstract of the U.S.* are combined here to define how capital punishment affects the poor and African-Americans.

Besides being an unfair alternative levied against the few, capital punishment is a very costly alternative. The actual cost of execution includes the price for defense and prosecuting attorneys, court costs, operating costs of super maximum-security units, and a share of top-level prison officials' time. David Lester, a professor of psychology and criminal justice, says that other costs processed through many different agencies must be considered as well, especially those from the extended appeals process, which may take 10 years or more. These court costs must be absorbed by different levels of government because as Congressman Clay explains, "less than 1 percent of over 2,000 inmates sitting on death row had legal counsel paid for by private funds. Over 99 percent of those awaiting execution are indigents who were represented by public defenders or counsel appointed by the courts" (145–46). A recent Duke University study estimated that the 56 executions in 1995 cost taxpayers $121 million (Dirnan). Finally, Sister Helen Prejean states that one prisoner on death row costs Louisiana over three million dollars (171). **(4)**

For these exorbitant costs, states are not getting a deterrent to crime. "Deterrence" refers to a circumstance in which an indi-

---

4. Here Zak uses quotations and paraphrases to discuss reasons for the high cost of capital punishment and then to provide specific estimates.

vidual refrains from an act because he or she perceives a risk of punishment for the act and fears that punishment. When the death penalty was instituted, one of the strongest supporting factors was that it would stop many people from killing others.

However, many experts claim that the threat of a death sentence does not lower the murder rate because murderers rarely weigh the costs of their actions. Mark Costanzo, author of *Just Revenge: Costs and Consequences of the Death Penalty*, claims that planned intentional murders make up less than 10 percent of the total. Discussing which would-be killers might be deterred by the threat of execution, he writes:

> Probably not the person who acts in the heat of passion or the person whose attempt at robbery goes tragically wrong. Certainly not the insane or mentally disturbed killer or the person whose mind is clouded by alcohol or drugs at the time of the murder. Not the young gang mamber whose whole subculture exalts macho displays and risk-taking. Not the person who kills spontaneously or accidentally in the midst of an altercation. (104–05)

Costanzo claims that more than one hundred years of experience and 200 research studies have shown that the death penalty does not act as an effective deterrent (103). In spite of such evidence, some death penalty supporters cite recent declines in the murder rate, yet, according to the Death Penalty Information Center, states with no death penalty have a lower average murder rate than those states with the death penalty, 3.5 per 100,000 population as compared to 6.6 per 100,000. **(5)**

Because of its real costs and ineffectiveness, the death penalty should be abolished in the United States. As a nation, we proclaim that we are the most advanced, most respected, most fair, and most civilized in the entire world. Having capital punishment is a direct contradiction of this proclamation. A much better alternative is life imprisonment without possibility of parole, which protects society from the offender and exacts a long, hard punishment, at a much lower cost. **(6)**

Works Cited

Brown, Edmund, and Dick Adler. *Public Justice, Private Mercy.* New York: Weidenfield, 1989.

Clay, William L. *To Kill or Not to Kill.* San Bernardino, CA: Borgo, 1990.

Costanzo, Mark. *Just Revenge: Costs and Consequences of the Death Penalty.* New York: St. Martin's, 1997.

Death Penalty Information Center. "Facts about Deterrence and the

---

5. The indented quotation explains why executions do not affect the murder rate.
6. The final paragraph provides Zak's alternative solution.

Death Penalty." 1997. 2 September 1998 <www.essential.org/dpic/

deter.html>.

Dirnan, Robert F. "Discriminatory, Costly, Death Penalty Lives

On." *National Catholic Reporter* 5 April 1996. 1 September 1998

<http://web7.searchbank.com/itw/session/178/8/29350074w3/

3!xm_5_5_A18202201>.

Lester, David. *The Death Penalty: Issues and Answers*. Springfield, IL: Tho-

mas, 1987.

Olson, Elizabeth. "U.N. Report Criticizes U.S. for 'Racist Use of Death

Penalty.'" *New York Times on the Web* 7 April 1998. 1 September

1998. <http://medusa/prod.oclc.org:3058/:next=NE...cs+1:/

fsrec7.txt%22%3Asessionid+3227542:7>.

Prejean, Helen. *Dead Man Walking*. New York: Random, 1983.

Quindlen, Anna. "Death Penalty's False Promise: An Eye for an Eye."

Elements of Argument. Ed. Annette T. Rottenberg. New York: St.

Martin's, 1990.

U.S. Bureau of Census. *Statistical Abstract of the United States: 1998*.

1998. 1 September 1998. <www.census.gov/prod/3/98pubs/98stabab/

$asec5.pdf>.

Zimring, Franklin E., and Gordon Hawkins. *Capital Punishment and the*

American Agenda. New York: Cambridge, 1986.

Chapter 8

Citing Print and Electronic Resources

Sarah Sheehan-Harris

Congratulations! Your paper is done! Almost.

But wait, there's more!

Just when you thought it was all over you must add one more page to your paper. The last page lists all the sources you used in your paper. These are called either citations or references.

WHY DO I NEED CITATIONS?

You must cite or reference every book, journal article, newspaper, Website, or other source you used to create your paper. In your paper you may have quoted directly from a source and you must give credit to the original author. Citations allow any person reading your paper to find the original sources you used.

Failing to give appropriate credit to the original author is called *plagiarism*. At most schools, if you are caught plagiarizing any portion of your paper you will fail the assignment and the course.

WHAT IS A CITATION?

A citation consists of the information needed to identify the work and where it can be found. Common items found in citations include:

Books	Journals
Author(s) or Editor(s)	Author(s)
Title	Article Title
Edition	Journal Title
Publisher	Volume Number
Place of Publication	Issue Number
Date	Page Numbers
	Date

WHAT IS A STYLE GUIDE?

Now, a style guide doesn't have anything to do with fashion. A *style guide* shows you exactly how your citations are to be placed in your paper. Also, a style guide will show you what size margins to use, how to set up the title page, and how to number the pages of your paper. These may seem like little things, but they do count toward the overall grade of your paper.

Your first step is to know exactly which style guide your instructor wants you to use. There are many different style guides available and specific ones are used for specific subjects. The two most commonly used style guides are:

- *Publication Manual of the American Psychological Association*, 4th edition (APA)
- *Modern Language Association Style Guide*, 5th edition (MLA)

Be sure you are using the most recent edition of the required style guide. There are changes in each new edition and your instructor may lower your grade for any inaccuracies in the style of your paper.

There are also many brief guides available on the Web that will show you how to reference or cite books and articles, using APA or MLA style. Unless they are published directly from the American Psychological Association or the Modern Language Association, you should avoid them.

BASIC CITATION FORMATS

When you quote directly from another source or you just use an article or book's idea, you will need to credit that person in the paper. You will need to cite the information used in your paper twice. First, at the place where you quoted or paraphrased the information. Second, you will also need to have a complete reference list of all the sources used at the end of your paper. Even if you did not directly quote from a source, if you used it, list it.

Both APA and MLA use parenthetical references for books and magazine articles that are directly quoted in your paper. A *parenthetical reference* is the author's last name and appropriate page number in parenthesis at the end of the quoted paragraph.

The following is a quote from an article about censorship on the Internet. This is how a parenthetical reference should look.

MLA

Filtering software sends the wrong message. It tells kids we do not trust them, that they can't make their own decisions, and that the computer knows what is good or bad for them (Nellen 53).

Author   **Page Number**

APA

Filtering software sends the wrong message. It tells kids we do not trust them, that they can't make their own decisions, and that the computer knows what is good or had for them (Nellen, 1998, p. 53).

Author   **Date**

Page Number

In MLA style, using authors' last names will lead the reader to the reference list or bibliography at the end of the paper. The page number then allows the reader to know exactly what page to find the idea or quote in the appropriate book or article.

In the APA style guide the date is also used. On occasion you may use two different sources from the same author and the date is a quick way to identify the correct one in the reference list.

REFERENCE LISTS

A reference list or bibliography is the last page of your paper. It will list the sources, books, articles, newspapers, and Websites that you used in your paper. All the sources listed parenthetically need to be included in the reference list. Remember, sources that you read but didn't quote from exactly must also be listed.

Sources are listed alphabetically by the author's last name. If there is more than one author, you must list each name.

The following are examples of how to list sources in your reference list. This is just a brief introduction. For a more in-depth explanation, please refer to the style guide recommended by your instructor.

SAMPLE CITATIONS

This section will show you examples of citations in a reference list for books and magazine (or journal) articles that are found in traditional print format. These citations are not used for books or magazine (or journal) articles found on the World Wide Web or through a Web-based periodical index.

MLA Citing a Book

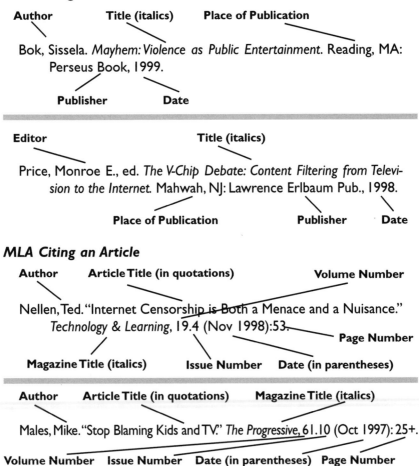

Author   **Title (italics)**   **Place of Publication**

Bok, Sissela. *Mayhem: Violence as Public Entertainment*. Reading, MA: Perseus Book, 1999.

Publisher   **Date**

Editor   **Title (italics)**

Price, Monroe E., ed. *The V-Chip Debate: Content Filtering from Television to the Internet.* Mahwah, NJ: Lawrence Erlbaum Pub., 1998.

Place of Publication   **Publisher**   **Date**

MLA Citing an Article

Author   **Article Title (in quotations)**   **Volume Number**

Nellen, Ted. "Internet Censorship is Both a Menace and a Nuisance." *Technology & Learning*, 19.4 (Nov 1998):53.

Page Number

Magazine Title (italics)   **Issue Number**   **Date (in parentheses)**

Author   **Article Title (in quotations)**   **Magazine Title (italics)**

Males, Mike. "Stop Blaming Kids and TV." *The Progressive*, 61.10 (Oct 1997): 25+.

Volume Number   **Issue Number**   **Date (in parentheses)**   **Page Number**

APA Citing a Book

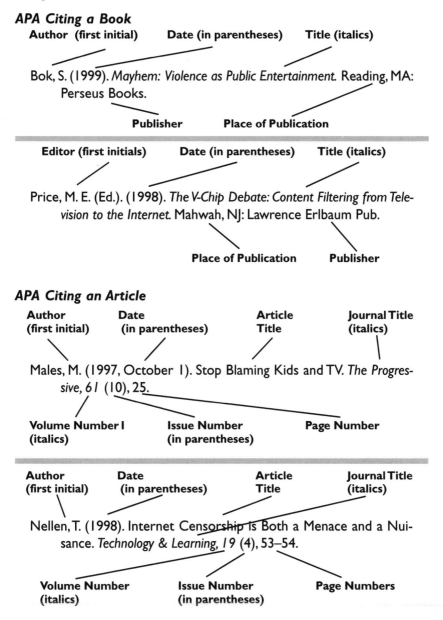

Author (first initial)   Date (in parentheses)   Title (italics)

Bok, S. (1999). *Mayhem: Violence as Public Entertainment.* Reading, MA: Perseus Books.

Publisher   Place of Publication

Editor (first initials)   Date (in parentheses)   Title (italics)

Price, M. E. (Ed.). (1998). *The V-Chip Debate: Content Filtering from Television to the Internet.* Mahwah, NJ: Lawrence Erlbaum Pub.

Place of Publication   Publisher

APA Citing an Article

Author (first initial)   Date (in parentheses)   Article Title   Journal Title (italics)

Males, M. (1997, October 1). Stop Blaming Kids and TV. *The Progressive, 61* (10), 25.

Volume Number (italics)   Issue Number (in parentheses)   Page Number

Author (first initial)   Date (in parentheses)   Article Title   Journal Title (italics)

Nellen, T. (1998). Internet Censorship Is Both a Menace and a Nuisance. *Technology & Learning, 19* (4), 53–54.

Volume Number (italics)   Issue Number (in parentheses)   Page Numbers

Now these examples just cover the basics. Other sources, such as reference books or books that are part of a series, make the citation more complicated. Check with your library about a copy of the style guide you are required to use about these changes. Or talk to your instructor about it.

CITING ELECTRONIC RESOURCES

If you found information for your paper or project using a World Wide Web resource, even if it is a book or magazine (or journal) article, you must include additional information in your citations. Just as with printed resources, MLA and APA have differences in citations for electronic resources.

MLA Citing a Web Page

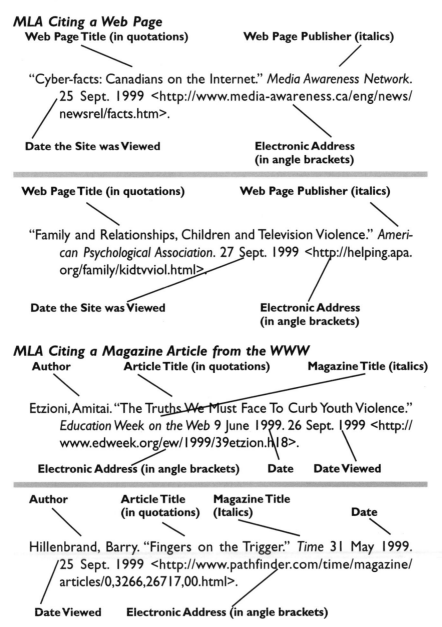

Web Page Title (in quotations)   Web Page Publisher (italics)

"Cyber-facts: Canadians on the Internet." *Media Awareness Network.* 25 Sept. 1999 <http://www.media-awareness.ca/eng/news/newsrel/facts.htm>.

Date the Site was Viewed   Electronic Address (in angle brackets)

Web Page Title (in quotations)   Web Page Publisher (italics)

"Family and Relationships, Children and Television Violence." *American Psychological Association.* 27 Sept. 1999 <http://helping.apa.org/family/kidtvviol.html>.

Date the Site was Viewed   Electronic Address (in angle brackets)

MLA Citing a Magazine Article from the WWW

Author   Article Title (in quotations)   Magazine Title (italics)

Etzioni, Amitai. "The Truths We Must Face To Curb Youth Violence." *Education Week on the Web* 9 June 1999. 26 Sept. 1999 <http://www.edweek.org/ew/1999/39etzion.h18>.

Electronic Address (in angle brackets)   Date   Date Viewed

Author   Article Title (in quotations)   Magazine Title (Italics)   Date

Hillenbrand, Barry. "Fingers on the Trigger." *Time* 31 May 1999. 25 Sept. 1999 <http://www.pathfinder.com/time/magazine/articles/0,3266,26717,00.html>.

Date Viewed   Electronic Address (in angle brackets)

MLA Citing an Article from a Library Database on the WWW

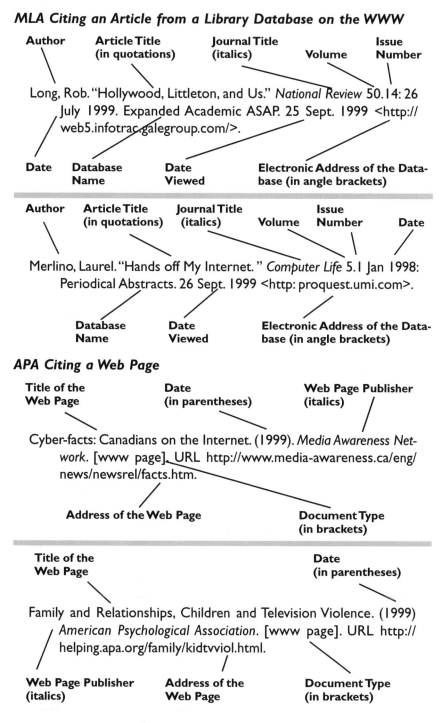

Author   Article Title   Journal Title   Issue
            (in quotations)   (italics)   Volume   Number

Long, Rob. "Hollywood, Littleton, and Us." *National Review* 50.14: 26
    July 1999. Expanded Academic ASAP. 25 Sept. 1999 <http://
    web5.infotrac.galegroup.com/>.

Date   Database   Date   Electronic Address of the Data-
         Name   Viewed   base (in angle brackets)

Author   Article Title   Journal Title   Issue
            (in quotations)   (italics)   Volume   Number   Date

Merlino, Laurel. "Hands off My Internet." *Computer Life* 5.1 Jan 1998:
    Periodical Abstracts. 26 Sept. 1999 <http: proquest.umi.com>.

Database   Date   Electronic Address of the Data-
Name   Viewed   base (in angle brackets)

APA Citing a Web Page

Title of the   Date   Web Page Publisher
Web Page   (in parentheses)   (italics)

Cyber-facts: Canadians on the Internet. (1999). *Media Awareness Net-*
    work. [www page]. URL http://www.media-awareness.ca/eng/
    news/newsrel/facts.htm.

Address of the Web Page   Document Type
                                       (in brackets)

Title of the   Date
Web Page   (in parentheses)

Family and Relationships, Children and Television Violence. (1999)
    American Psychological Association. [www page]. URL http://
    helping.apa.org/family/kidtvviol.html.

Web Page Publisher   Address of the   Document Type
(italics)   Web Page   (in brackets)

APA Citing a Magazine Article from the WWW

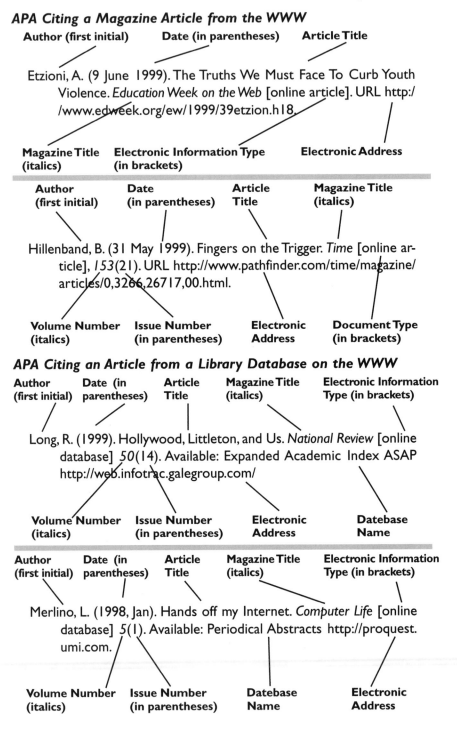

Author (first initial)   Date (in parentheses)   Article Title

Etzioni, A. (9 June 1999). The Truths We Must Face To Curb Youth
Violence. *Education Week on the Web* [online article]. URL http:/
/www.edweek.org/ew/1999/39etzion.h18.

Magazine Title   Electronic Information Type   Electronic Address
(italics)   (in brackets)

Author   Date   Article   Magazine Title
(first initial)   (in parentheses)   Title   (italics)

Hillenband, B. (31 May 1999). Fingers on the Trigger. *Time* [online ar-
ticle], *153*(21). URL http://www.pathfinder.com/time/magazine/
articles/0,3266,26717,00.html.

Volume Number   Issue Number   Electronic   Document Type
(italics)   (in parentheses)   Address   (in brackets)

APA Citing an Article from a Library Database on the WWW

Author   Date (in   Article   Magazine Title   Electronic Information
(first initial)   parentheses)   Title   (italics)   Type (in brackets)

Long, R. (1999). Hollywood, Littleton, and Us. *National Review* [online
database] *50*(14). Available: Expanded Academic Index ASAP
http://web.infotrac.galegroup.com/

Volume Number   Issue Number   Electronic   Datebase
(italics)   (in parentheses)   Address   Name

Author   Date (in   Article   Magazine Title   Electronic Information
(first initial)   parentheses)   Title   (italics)   Type (in brackets)

Merlino, L. (1998, Jan). Hands off my Internet. *Computer Life* [online
database] *5*(1). Available: Periodical Abstracts http://proquest.
umi.com.

Volume Number   Issue Number   Datebase   Electronic
(italics)   (in parentheses)   Name   Address

SAMPLE REFERENCE LISTS

The following sample reference list contains citations for a paper on the popularity of professional wrestling. Here are the types of sources listed in the order they appear.

1. Journal article read in the library
2. Book
3. Association Web page
4. Journal article printed out from a Web-based library database
5. Journal article read in the library
6. Book
7. Magazine article read from the magazine's Web page

MLA Reference List

Campbell, John W. "Professional Wrestling: Why the Bad Guy Wins." *Journal of American Culture* 19.2 (1996): 127–133.

Greenberg, Keith Elliot. *History of Pro Wrestling: From Carnivals to Cable TV*. Minneapolis: LernerSports, 2000.

"Home Page." *World Wrestling Federation*. 3 Oct. 1999 <http://www.wwf.com>.

Lemish, Dafna. "'Girls Can Wrestle Too': Gender Differences in the Consumption of a Television Wrestling Series." *Sex Roles: A Journal of Research* 38 (1998): 833+. Expanded Academic Index ASAP. 3 Oct. 1999 <http://web5.infotrac.galegroup.com/>.

May, Vaughn. "Cultural Politics and Professional Wrestling." *Studies in Popular Culture* 21.3 (1999): 79.

Mazor, Sharon. *Professional Wrestling: Sport and Spectacle*. Jackson: UP of Mississippi, 1998.

Rosellini, Lynn. "Lords of the Ring." *US News and World Report* 17 May 1999. 4 Oct 1999 <http://www.usnews.com/usnews/issue/990517/wrestling.htm>.

APA Reference List

Campbell, J. W. (1996). Professional Wrestling: Why the Bad Guy Wins. *Journal of American Culture 19*(2), 127–133.

Greenberg, K. E. (2000). *History of Pro Wrestling: From Carnivals to Cable TV*. Minneapolis, MN: LernerSports.

Home Page. (1999). *World Wrestling Federation*. [www page]. URL http://www.wwf.com.

Lemish, D. (1998). "Girls Can Wrestle Too: Gender Differences in the

Consumption of a Television Wrestling Series." *Sex Roles: A Journal of Research* [online database] *38*. Available: Expanded Academic Index ASAP <http://web5.infotrac.galegroup.com/>.

May, Vaughn. (1999). Cultural Politics and Professional Wrestling. *Studies in Popular Culture 21*(3), 79.

Mazor, S. (1998). *Professional Wrestling: Sport and Spectacle.* Jackson, MS: University Press of Mississippi.

Rosellini, Lynn. (17 May 1999). Lords of the Ring. *US News and World Report.* [online article] Available: http://www.usnews.com/usnews/issue/990517/wrestling.htm.

THE END (REALLY)

Congratulations! *Now* you're finished with your paper!

These are just a few examples of common sources found in a reference list or bibliography. Check with the specific style manual your instructor requires for sources not shown here.

Good Luck!

REFERENCE LIST

(You know I have to do one too!)

NOTE: The citations in this reference list are presented in the respective styles of APA and MLA.

American Psychological Association. (1994). *Publication Manual of the American Psychological Association* (4th ed.). Washington: American Psychological Association.

Gibaldi, J. (1999). *MLA Handbook for Writers of Research Papers* (5th ed.). New York: Modern Language Association of America.

About the Authors and the Editor

John L. Adams is an instructor of English at Loyola University in New Orleans. He has published articles in the *Journal of Teaching Writing, Rhetoric Society Quarterly, The Writing Instructor*, and other journals. His books include *The Accomplished Writer* and *Teaching Advanced Composition: Why and How*. His coauthored chapter on using creative writing pedagogies appeared in *Intersections: Theory-Practice in the Writing Center*.

Katherine H. Adams is a professor of English at Loyola University in New Orleans. She has published articles in *College Composition and Communication, Rhetoric Review, Teaching English in the Two-Year College, The Writing Instructor*, and other journals. Her books include *The Accomplished Writer, Easy Access: The Reference Handbook for Writers* (with Michael L. Keene), *A History of Professional Writing Instruction in American Colleges, Progressive Politics and the Training of America's Persuaders, Research and Writing Across the Disciplines* (with Michael L. Keene), and *Teaching Advanced Composition: Why and How*. She has recently finished *A Group of Their Own: How Professional Writing Became a Choice for American Women* (upcoming from SUNY Press), and she is currently working on a book concerning portrayals of women in newspaper stories.

Lara Bushallow is currently a systems librarian at George Mason University in Fairfax, Virginia. She received her MS in Library Science from the University of Buffalo in addition to her BA in Interdisciplinary Studies. Lara is a member of the American Library Association and chair of the Association of College and Research Libraries Committee on the Status of Academic Librarians.

Charles Harmon is director of publishing for Neal-Schuman Publishers, Inc. He holds a BA in English from High Point College and a master's degree in library science from the University of North Carolina–Greensboro. He has taught high school English and has worked in public, school, and special libraries.

Frederick D. King earned his master's degree in library science from The Catholic University of America School of Library and Information Science. Currently, he is the director of the Sr. Rosemary Donley Technology Center at the Catholic University School of Nursing (*http:// nursing.cua.edu*) and Webmaster for the Americans with Disabilities Act Program Assistance Coordinator project (*www.adata.org*). He has worked for the American Library Association and the Library of Congress and has taught at the Catholic University School of Library Science. He lives in Silver Spring, Maryland, with his books, computers, and tropical fish. In his spare time, he enjoys book collecting, hiking, and other activities that have nothing to do with computers.

Sarah Sheehan-Harris completed her BA in English and MS in Library Science at The Catholic University of America. She is a member of the Maryland Library Association and the Association of College and Research Libraries, Instruction Section. Currently working at George Mason University as the education and psychology reference liaison librarian, Sarah has also worked at the University of Maryland, Baltimore County, Frostburg State University, and the University of Maryland University College.

Index